Australian-born **Max Meyers** learnt to fly at sixteen. After seven years as a military pilot, he spent thirty-seven years in Mission Aviation Fellowship, seven years as CEO of MAF Australia and thirteen as President/CEO of MAF USA. An author and sought-after speaker, Max works today with leaders of developing world churches and Christian organisations through Development Associates International. He and his wife Jo now live in Colorado Springs and Melbourne.

Eyes Turned Skyward

A catalogue record for this book is available from the British Library.

ISBN 978-1-905991-43-3

Published by Mission Aviation Fellowship UK
Castle House, Castle Hill Avenue, Folkestone, Kent, UK CT20 2TN
Telephone: 0845 850 9505
Email: supporter.relations@maf-uk.org
Website: www.maf-uk.org

Mission Aviation Fellowship UK is a member of Mission Aviation Fellowship International.

Produced by New Wine Ministries.

Further copies can be obtained directly from MAF UK.

Cover picture: An MAF Cessna 206 aircraft at Iropena, in the highlands of Papua New Guinea
Photographer: Nels Kristenson

Typeset by CRB Associates, Potterhanworth, Lincolnshire, UK.
Printed in Scotland

Contents

A Note from the Author

How many men, I often wonder, experience the rare and delightful privilege of living out a childhood dream? Let alone the joy and fulfilment of discovering, as time goes by, that imbedded in those same boyhood ambitions is the very providence and purpose of God.

In the beginning, for me at least, it was all about aeroplanes. While World War II raged, the skies of Sydney were filled with the thundering roar of aircraft of every imaginable size and shape. I was completely and irreversibly hooked. "One day," I promised myself, "that will be me!" I just had to fly!

Later, as a teenager in a family where God was honoured, a troubling question tugged at my ambitions. If flying was for me – then how could I possibly reconcile such a deep passion with the undeniable conviction that God, too, had a deeper, higher and prior claim upon my life? If I yielded to the prompting of the Spirit, what would happen to my dream?

However, not unlike Peter and John of so long ago, rather than simply being asked to leave my 'nets' of ambition behind, I was sensing the gentle and yet life-transforming call: "Pick *up* your nets. Come, follow me."

A boyhood dream became a wondrous reality.

What follows, then, are simply stories. These stories are selected from my two books, *Riding the Heavens* and *On the Wings of the Dawn*, published in the USA by Zondervan Publishing House in 2000 and 2001. Here, they are presented for the first time for a UK audience as a single volume under a new title.

I was musing about a new title and thinking about how, long before any man had ever tasted the wonder of flight, Leonardo da Vinci wrote, "Once you have tasted flight, you will ever walk the earth with eyes turned skyward, for there you have been, and there you will always long to return."

From childhood, with a driving ambition to fly, I have walked "with eyes turned skyward".

As you read my stories, may your eyes be turned skyward too. See how God has used the technology of aviation to build and grow His Kingdom. But, as you read, may your eyes be turned beyond the sky . . . to the heavens.

Isaiah tells us that God "sits enthroned above the circle of the earth." Then he invites us to, "Lift your eyes and look to the heavens: Who created all these? He who brings out the starry host one by one, and calls them each by name."

May you see Him in the reading of this book. May these stories draw you closer to Jesus.

Max Meyers

PROLOGUE
A Higher Plane

*When I consider your heavens, the work of your fingers,
the moon and the stars, which you have set in place, what
is man that you are mindful of him, the son of man that
you care for him?*

Psalm 8:3–4

The sky was to be mine alone that night.

Tanks brimming with fuel, my Gloster Meteor F8 jet fighter sat low and heavy, its military-grey coat a perfect camouflage against the winter's night. I fumbled with my flashlight. The rain and wind made pre-flight inspection difficult and uncomfortable.

Releasing the bubble canopy, I climbed into the aircraft and settled into my seat.

After the customary check around the cockpit and a 'thumbs-up' to the waiting crew chief, I flipped the starter switch for the left-hand engine and listened for the reassuring whine of the compressor. The instruments flickered into life – RPM, oil pressure, jet pipe temperature, fuel flow. Anticipating the unmistakable deep-throated rumble of ignition, I repeated the procedure on the right engine. With the wheel chocks removed, all was ready.

I could not have known that this rather routine flight would give rise to a most memorable experience.

The penetrating beam of the nose light pierced the darkness and illuminated the driving rain. I followed the diffused lights of the taxiway into the night. Completing the final memorised checklist 'on the run' and positioning the aircraft on the runway centre line, I held it stationary with the brakes.

I opened the throttles with my left hand and gripped the brake lever with my right. The two jet engines responded with a familiar, throaty roar as the power increased. The plane strained, eager to fly. Exhilaration. Energy brought to life with the left hand, held captive with the right.

Taking a breath, I released the brakes and, like a sprinter from the blocks, the plane leapt forward, pressing me back: seventy-five knots . . . ninety knots . . . ease back on the column . . . nose wheel off . . . a hundred and twenty knots . . . airborne . . . undercarriage retracted . . . climbing speed.

I began scanning the instruments and in a matter of seconds was enveloped by heavy clouds, immediately encountering the violent buffeting and turbulence that gives thunderstorms their notoriety amongst aviators. The ferocity of the storm surprised me. My three-ton aircraft was being tossed and thrown about. I marvelled at the energy and power of just one winter storm. Not a good night to fly!

Suddenly, at thirty-five thousand feet I burst into the blackness above the clouds.

The night sky was brilliantly clear. The stars were clusters of bright light. It seemed I could reach out and clutch them, one by one. Below, the earth was totally obscured by a soft pewter-grey blanket of cloud. With the stars as my close and sole companions, I turned on to heading, my frustrations with the weather gone, my regrets forgotten.

Soon I was hard at work, leaving the stars to their own

beauty. I concentrated on the task of successfully completing what was a navigational exercise.

Fifty minutes later, high over the western reaches of Australia's New South Wales, the exercise was finished. I had reached the third and final checkpoint on time and with reasonable accuracy. It was now simply a matter of flying home. The pressure was off. It was time to relax!

Heading east, I looked up through the clear canopy to survey again the beauty of the night sky. Tuning the radio from the repetitive 'dots and dashes' of the navigational beacons I had been using, I found a pleasant, all-night classical music station. With the roar of the engines left far behind, the soft and lovely strains of a string quartet somehow matched the night!

But my memory of that night was to change forever. It was barely discernible at first. Far ahead, increasing in intensity as the minutes ticked by, a blood-red horizontal line appeared against the blackness of the sky.

Away to the south I noticed another line, that same brilliant red, not straight like the first but curled and irregular, arching high into the atmosphere.

What followed was a stunning display of colour, a gradual progression to pink, then a softening to warm orange and gold. This amazing light, whose source lay far beyond the horizon, chased away the blackness of the night and yet did not in the slightest way diminish the brilliance of the stars. The curled, irregular line to the south became the outline of a towering, cumulonimbus cloud, awash in the same spectacular variegation of red, pink, orange and gold. An awesome sight.

I realised, then, what it was – this glorious display of changing colour. I smiled.

This was no extraordinary stellar phenomenon. Nothing so rare as the aurora australis or the northern lights.

It was simply the rising of the moon.

The minutes went by. Before long the picture was complete. The first golden arc of the moon broke the horizon and then, full and round, it climbed quickly into the blackness of the night. The more vivid colours gone, its magnificent now-silver glow laced the cloud and filled the eastern sky with a warm lustre.

I gazed in awe through the fighter's gunsight and the front panels of the cockpit windscreen. This night's moon seemed different. It was not the same familiar 'passer-by' in the sky. This shining satellite of the earth seemed so close, as if its silken dusty face was to be my landing place. It was a gigantic, round, silver ball, a massive, pock-marked inanimate thing of beauty moving silently, inexorably higher on its journey in space.

Fighter flying is a rather macho business, but this was no macho moment. This was an experience of pure emotion, of pure romance. Turning down the volume control of the radio, I watched in awed silence. To share this moment, so extraordinary and glorious, even with music, was to diminish its splendour.

And, as I gazed, mesmerised at what was before me, a deepening sense of awe and wonder dawned. I was seeing God at work. And He was showing something indescribably beautiful. To me alone. No one else that night on a cloud-enshrouded earth would see what I had seen. I was an audience of one for this amazing demonstration of God's creative genius.

The King and I!

Marvellous words about Him from the Psalms burst into my mind. Other verses followed, familiar since childhood but now imbued with fresh and vibrant significance.

The heavens declare the glory of God; the skies proclaim the work of his hands.

Psalm 19:1

*When I consider your heavens, the work of your fingers,
the moon and the stars, which you have set in place, what
is man that you are mindful of him, the son of man that
you care for him?*

Psalm 8:3–4

There, alone with God, I worshipped Him, deeply and emotionally, perhaps in a way I had never done before. I considered
the glory of God the Creator. Who was I in the light of that
glory? What really is man when he considers the moon and
the stars, which God has made?

I had known about God all my life. I had known Him –
personally, relationally – ever since teenage years. But at that
freeze-moment in time, audience to an astounding demonstration of His glory and creative genius, the wonder of a
personal relationship became infinitely more precious. The
irony of it all – the smallness, the weakness, the fragility
of my humanity, especially as I was squeezed into the restric-
tive cockpit of a modern-day jet fighter plane. It seemed
unspeakable that a connection could ever be made between
such a God and myself, yet I knew it was real. He created
the connection. He built the bridge – because He loved
me. The same power source that brought into being this
magnificent silver ball in the sky ahead and placed it in its
precise and totally ordered orbit also reached out in love to
me and made me His child. He had even said that I could
call him "Father".

I couldn't kneel; I couldn't close my eyes. At least not just
then. My heart, indeed my very spirit, sang in delightful
harmony, at one with God. A solitary jet fighter plane became
my strange and beautiful cathedral, the ejection seat my pew.
I felt safe there, cradled, held in a security beyond compare.

I belonged to this master painter, this creative genius. He
held me firmly, safely, lovingly.

5

I closed my eyes then, and worshipped. Alone, but not alone.

Now, I reflect with nostalgia on that glorious, stormy night so long ago. And I am reminded of a challenge it held for me. A simple challenge. Clear. Direct.

"Come. Follow me!"

It demanded a response. It still does.

PART 1

1

The Stuff of Dreams

How great is the love the Father has lavished on us, that
we should be called children of God!

1 John 3:1

Life can be pretty boring for a kid.

But sometimes, gloriously unexpected things happen.

Such was the day for me when I took my first ride in an aeroplane.

From earliest childhood I had turned my eyes to the sky at the sound of every plane. In the forties our family lived in 'safe' Sydney. The most we saw of World War II were the aircraft that flew overhead. I loved to hear the screaming howls of their engines. I loved to watch as they practised their incredible dogfight manoeuvres high above. From the ground they were black specks against the blue. But there were men up there. And I was a boy. And it all seemed a great adventure to me.

I clearly recall one particular day when my brothers and I sat under the wing of a grey-green Dakota at Sydney's Mascot Airport. It was parked with two others, right by the fence on the far boundary. Each of them bore the insignia of the Royal Dutch Air Force. The crew members appeared to have little to do but lounge around by their aircraft. Only young men, their stories amazed us. Evading the Japanese army as it stormed its way through Java, down towards Australia, they had flown from the Dutch East Indies and were simply hanging out, far from home, awaiting reassignment. We sat open-mouthed, listening to their tales.

In the evenings, with our parents, we crowded around the radio as Dad twiddled the dial to catch, through the crackle and static, the news of the war. We heard of the exploits of men like these – in New Guinea and other war zones in the Pacific region.

Aeroplanes – flying! Unbelievable adventure. Uniformed men with wings on their chests. The heroes of the day.

To fly! This was the stuff of dreams.

And then the war was over and life slowly returned to normal. On my street, dads and elder brothers returned. Most of them.

The decade drew to a close. There were very few military planes to watch anymore. The grey-green Dakotas of wartime had become the shiny silver airliners that now flew overhead. But dreams never die.

I thought my dad was the best dad on the street. But he was always busy. He worked long hours, and it seemed that there were so many things that needed his attention, especially on weekends. There were few family outings. And family vacations were rare. There was no time, and no extra money. On a Saturday, he could be something of a slave-driver, demanding our help to get those jobs done. We, of course, would rather have been skinny-dipping in the forbidden quarry or smoking home-rolled newspaper cigarettes in our secret hiding place underneath the wooden floor of the local church.

Sundays were 'church days'. Church in the morning. Church in the afternoon. Church at supper time. It seemed to me that we were a 'churched-out' family!

Then one day, late in 1949, Dad announced that he had been able to get some time off work and was planning to take the family away on holiday. It was to be at a place he had often talked about, by the beach. There would be sand dunes to climb, bush to explore! We could swim at either the surf beach or in a still-water lake behind the sand dunes. It sounded absolutely fantastic.

But after supper, my parents said to me, "Hey, Max, don't leave the table yet. We need to talk with you about this holiday." I was a little apprehensive. Special talks usually involved reprimand or punishment. But this time there was no hint of impending trouble for me in their voices, rather, a sympathetic tone.

"This is going to be really tough on you, Son," my dad said. "You'll have to stay at home while we take the other kids on this holiday. The only vacation time I can get is right when you'll be doing the Intermediate Exam. Any other year it wouldn't matter quite as much, but this year it's different. You just can't be away. I've tried hard to change the dates, but it simply isn't possible. You'll have to stay here with Grandma while we're gone."

There was genuine sadness in their eyes as they told me how much they had tried to make it work for us all to be together.

Stay at home? Miss such an exciting place? When everyone else was going? The only one of all five kids not to go? I argued with them that the Intermediate Exam wasn't really important. But to no avail. There would be no vacation at all for anyone that year if, because of me, the holiday was cancelled.

I really did understand, and I knew it had to be. But there was mileage to be made out of the situation, so I didn't try to hide my disappointment.

"I promise you, Son, that we'll do something special just for you. Something that will help make up for this. I don't know what it'll be yet, but I promise you it'll be really good." But how could anything make up for missing two weeks at the beach? I couldn't think of anything that could be that special!

I waved them goodbye. That was easy. And Grandma really spoiled me while they were away. She felt bad for me too. It was their coming home that hurt. Their sunburned faces, the stories they recounted, tales of fishing, swimming, exploring – they had had a wonderful time. I sat, feeling excluded, listening enviously. What 'special thing' could ever possibly make up for such a loss?

A few weeks passed. The exams were over. Conversation about the marvellous vacation had become sporadic.

Then, one evening, Dad spoke to me. "Max, I've worked out what you and I are going to do. I'm going to take you, in an aeroplane, to Canberra."

"What?"

I stared at him. Had I heard him correctly? Did he say . . . ? I couldn't believe it! An aeroplane!

Absolutely nothing could have generated such joy for me. How could they possibly have conceived of an idea so utterly fantastic? My wildest dreams. How could they afford it?

Dad continued. He spoke about Canberra, as if that might be the highlight of this wonderful proposal. "It's the national capital. A city built and designed specifically for that reason. We'll go to Parliament House, to the National War Museum, to the Institute of Anatomy. I've booked the first flight in the day for us and the last flight home. It should be a great time."

Frankly, I didn't care much for parliament houses or war museums. Certainly not for institutes of anatomy. But – to go in an aeroplane? Wow! Who wouldn't give up two weeks of family vacation for that?

The great day came. Dad had the airline tickets safely in his inside pocket. It was dark when we left home to walk to the bus stop and still dark when we reached the station and caught the train into Sydney. Even now, I can remember my pride as I strutted with my father into the city terminal of Australian National Airways,

"Man!" I thought to myself, "I've got a great dad!"

"The bus in the first bay is for passengers to Canberra," announced the voice on the public address system. I walked out and boarded, the only kid among a group of businessmen. I felt ten feet tall. Even the ride to the airport was exciting. I wanted everyone who saw that airline bus go by to notice me. I was going flying!

And there it stood. That shiny, beautiful Douglas DC-3, glistening in the early morning sunlight. A company flag flew from a small mast near the captain's window. 'Australian National Airlines' was written in red along the fuselage. Men were loading luggage into its freight bay behind the passenger door. Others fuelled it from a large tanker truck. A uniformed stewardess then walked across the tarmac and stood by the stairway.

What an aircraft! It was identical in shape to the old khaki-green Dutch Dakotas that had fascinated us as small boys all those years ago. Only this one was different. This was a flagship. This was unique. This one was mine.

Carpet on the floor. Luxurious leather seats.

The aisle seemed very steep. There were rows of two seats on one side, one on the other. We were shown to our assigned places a little way up the aircraft, just behind the wing. My dad sat by the aisle. The window seat was mine.

I could see such pleasure in Dad's eyes as I poured my excitement over him and thanked him for bringing me on this incredible adventure. How could he have known? Had he and my mum been able to see inside my heart, they could not have found an experience to match this one. What a prize – just for staying home from a family vacation!

The door was closed and all was ready. With a peculiar whine, the right-hand propeller began to turn, then there was a loud noise as the engine started. The white smoke that poured out of the cowls was whisked away by the slipstream. Then the other engine started. The plane vibrated, jerked a little, and moved forward. The pilot turned it sharply and began to taxi towards the take-off point.

The stewardess walked up and down the aisle, offering sweets to each of the passengers and checking that all seatbelts were securely fastened. We were on our way!

The engines roared. The vibration increased. And with a jerk the take-off roll began. Faster and faster. The steep aisle became level as the tail came up. The grass at the side of the airstrip flashed by, faster and faster, and then – it just dropped away, downwards and backwards! We were flying!

I'm sure I never even noticed the cold glass as I pressed my face against the window. Soon the horizon on my side of the plane rose ever higher as the wing came down, and we circled the airport. I could see the outline of Sydney, with its tall buildings, beautiful glistening harbour, the famous Sydney Harbour bridge and, far away, the ocean.

Flying!

My dad's face was close to mine as we peered out of that square window. He had only flown once before, back in the early thirties. It had been from that same airport. He had saved up his pocket money and taken a joyride in an old barnstorming biplane. So he was excited too! But I think he enjoyed my excitement even more as he shared my great adventure.

We saw the red roofs of Sydney's houses. We saw fields and trees and tiny cars – and even tinier people. I felt a pressure in my ears and a strange feeling in my stomach as our shiny silver bird climbed upwards to make its way to Canberra.

What a morning that was! We flew on for about an hour. Then the feeling in my ears told me that we were coming down. The ground was getting closer and closer. The tyres squealed as we landed at Canberra. Back to earth again.

The War Museum was much better than I had expected. I particularly remember the Lancaster bomber and the Spitfire and the other warplanes of renown on display. Polished and clean, the objects of my awe and passion. So close I could almost touch them.

Parliament House didn't impress me much. As we looked down from the visitors' gallery, it seemed to me that those politicians were just a bunch of men in church clothes shouting at one another – all at once! All I remember about the Institute of Anatomy is row upon row of jars containing pickled pieces of people!

By mid-afternoon I was fidgeting. *Let's get back in the air again, I thought impatiently.*

I couldn't appropriately express to my dad how I felt about what he had done for me – something so unbelievably wonderful. My "thank you" seemed quite inadequate. I remember taking his hand as we walked across the tarmac that evening back in Sydney. I had thought myself too old to hold my dad's hand. That was for little kids. But not on this day. This was different. This was a hand-holding day!

I sensed his deep, smiling pleasure.

What a day it had been!

But neither of us knew what a milestone it had really been in my life. A crossroads. A significant intersection.

I write this story sitting in the terminal of the crowded San Francisco Airport. A huge Japan Airlines Boeing 747 is taxiing by. It probably has four hundred people on board. Farther across the tarmac I see planes from Germany, Britain, Thailand, Hong Kong and, of course, dozens of US domestic jets.

I don't see a single DC-3.

Passengers by the thousands scurry from gate to gate. Others sit bored-looking, waiting for their flight to be called. Some are using laptop computers, others scratching away on their Palm Pilots. There are kids too. Hundreds of them – but none of them seem excited. Out on the tarmac, airline employees are racing around each other in tiny tractors, some with luggage carts snaking along behind. I don't see a single fuel truck.

This isn't Mascot, and the thrill is missing. Things have changed. People seldom walk out across the tarmac to their planes any more. Stewardesses rarely stand in the breeze by the stairway.

I recall a lifetime of years involved in aviation. I see myself now, an ageing man who has spent thousands of hours sitting in planes as a passenger. Then, looking back a few years, I see a much younger man flying hundreds of different aircraft, and I have a vision of piles of logbooks filled with records of almost twelve thousand hours I have flown as a pilot. Then I see a sixteen-year-old going solo for the first time, and a fourteen-year-old leaving school to work and earn enough money to fulfil his dream of learning to fly. And finally I see that wide-eyed, awestruck young boy taking his first flight in a shiny DC-3.

But I see something else. Someone else. I see my dad.

I see his smile. I sense his love. I feel his pleasure. And I grasp his hand once again.

The joy comes back – and I feel a little like crying. My dad has long since gone to be in heaven with Jesus, but it feels as if he is sitting here with me, smiling again as I write his story.

And I feel the love of another Father as well. A Heavenly Father who, aeons ago, planned that day for me. I feel His hand in mine too. He had things ahead for me of which I could only dream – a unique plan for my life. I had my first glimpse of it that day. That boyhood flight in an ex-military DC-3 heralded a lifetime of adventure beyond my wildest dreams. My Heavenly Father gave to my earthly father the joy of sharing the moment when I first realised that my cherished dreams could become reality.

Tears come to my eyes when I think of that Heavenly Father as well. Tears of gratitude and love for what He has allowed my life to be.

It feels as if my dad is here with me today, watching the hustle and bustle of this modern airport. And so is the God of creation, the Master of the universe. I'm so glad that all my days were ordained for me. Especially that one.

2

Too Close for Comfort

Timothy, guard what has been entrusted to your care.
1 Timothy 6:20

Death was seconds away.

My Meteor was hurtling, almost vertically, downwards. The ground was racing closer and closer at a frightening rate. I didn't dare look at the air speed indicator, but the needle must have been right up against the red arc – well in excess of five hundred and fifty knots. I did see the altimeter winding down like a clock gone mad. Both throttles were closed, the air brakes deployed, but it seemed as if the plane was still accelerating. I was pulling the control column with both hands, with all my might, back into my stomach.

"God, I'm not going to make it!"

There was a very slight change in attitude. The nose began to rise. But there was no change in the aircraft's direction. It was heading straight towards the ground.

No response.

In my frantic attempts to raise the nose of the aircraft, my arms and head felt like lead, my body as if it weighed a ton. The G-force was extreme. With mouth wide open under my oxygen mask, I was groaning aloud, pleading with the aircraft to recover. It felt as if my cheeks were against my chest, my eyeballs almost popping out of their sockets.

The difference between life and death would be measured in microseconds. But the choice had been made. And there was absolutely nothing more I could do about it. I was far too low to attempt ejection. I knew death was approaching at a horrifying pace. I had heard that time seems to expand under such circumstances. It certainly did for me that day. Ironically, it seemed my thoughts were crystal clear and almost in slow motion. I recall being utterly furious with myself.

I'll end up just like Harry, I thought, *and I can do nothing about it.*

In my mind I saw again the image of a huge, irregular hole in the ground, about forty miles from my base, where a couple of months earlier Harry's Meteor had buried itself with incredible force into a farmer's field during a night exercise. A few days later, as we solemnly carried Harry's coffin at the military funeral, we all knew that the heavy weight on our shoulders was artificial. The only remains left of our friend would have fitted into a shoe box.

"You fool!" was my desperate cry as that terrible dive continued. "You utterly stupid fool. Your life . . . your mission . . . all gone . . . through absolute recklessness."

I can't remember the final moments of that deadly descent or the recovery from it. I had totally blacked out. My first recollection is of the instrument panel slowly reappearing, as through a thick fog. The altimeter needle was turning clockwise now, indicating that I was climbing again. But with no power from the two engines, and the speed brakes still deployed, the air speed was quickly deteriorating. The aircraft was on the point of stall.

I rolled the plane over to level flight, applied power to the engines, retracted the speed brakes, and ran through a checklist to ensure that all was well. Everything seemed okay. I sat, shocked, pale and breathing heavily. I blinked my eyes, clawing my way back to full consciousness.

Somehow I had got through.

I nursed the jet home gently. After shutdown, I reported to the engineering officer that it had almost certainly been over-stressed and would need a thorough check-up. I didn't speak to anybody in the crew room. I just signed off the flight sheet, got into my car, and drove back to my quarters. I was so ashamed of my foolishness. I found myself confessing to God how close I had come to ruining my life. I thought of my family, my parents, my siblings . . . and the anguish there would have been in our home. I castigated myself for running so perilously close to death and jeopardising all I believed life held for me in the days and years ahead – God's plans for me.

The rest of the afternoon was spent in a sombre and sober mood. The ramifications of my actions raced around my mind. Over and over again. How could I have let myself be so irresponsible?

The flight had been listed on the squadron operations sheet as 'Army Co-op'. I'd been doing it for the entire week. The first few runs had been fun and not overly demanding. The object of the exercise was to train young army officers in how to call for air support when engaged in ground battle. These simulated exercises were usually conducted on huge military reserves north-west of Sydney. I would be given co-ordinates to identify the general position of the army group and then fly into the area to await the radio call from the instructor. One by one, the trainees would take the micro-phone, identify the type of attack they wanted, the weapon required, and give the co-ordinates for the target.

It might be something like, "Para 35, request rocket attack on a bridge, co-ordinates Tango Romeo Echo One Six. Advise commencing attack." Once the target was identified, the aircraft was positioned to roll into the dive and carry out the most efficient attack possible. Pulling out of the dive would be at a prescribed height. There was no danger to anyone on the ground, nor to the aircraft – assuming minimums were adhered to.

Thus, up and down I would go. From twenty-five thousand feet . . . down to five hundred feet. Twenty-five thousand feet . . . five hundred feet. Again and again. Over and over.

After a while it really became quite monotonous, which was why no one on the squadron fought to be assigned to this role. We all much preferred firing 'live' weapons on a gunnery range or attempting to shoot each other down in air-to-air combat training. We even preferred the scenery of a high- or low-level cross-country flight. And this day was the last day of my week-long assignment to army co-op. I was glad it would soon be over.

It had been on the second to last attack, while at the bottom of a dive and rather close to the ground, that I saw, for the first time, the men who were actually making these requests of me. Usually they remained undetected. But there they were. A couple of khaki-coloured jeeps with long antennae and a squad of military personnel in camouflage fatigues. They were clustered together beneath some trees. I marked their position on the map.

"I'll give you some hurry-up before we're through today!" I said to myself.

At the completion of the last of the simulated attacks I climbed to twenty-five thousand feet. The call came.

"Para 35, you're clear to base. That's all we want. Thanks. Out." This was my chance.

"Out, eh? Not likely," I muttered to myself. "You're not finished with me yet. You blokes have kept me doing this all week. Now it's my turn! And hang the five-hundred-foot minimum!"

I rolled the aircraft on to its back, to them a tiny speck in the sky far above. Applying full throttle to gain some speed, I began my twenty-five-thousand-foot, near-vertical dive. In seconds I had the jeeps in my gunsight. They loomed larger and larger as the plane screamed towards the ground.

Attack dives were never as steep as this. So my pull-out point was more a matter of guesswork than procedure. *Now! Now! Pull out now*, I thought. But I was determined to give these soldiers something to remember. And the seconds ticked by. Precious seconds.

The very instant I initiated recovery from my near-vertical dive, I knew I had left it too late. I pulled back with all my might on the control column, applied the speed brakes, and slammed the throttles closed. But nothing happened. I plummeted earthwards.

The Meteor, at a high dive speed, sometimes displayed a peculiar characteristic. It would change attitude but not direction. So, while the nose of the aircraft was beginning to rise, the aircraft itself was actually continuing downwards, 'squashing', in a screaming vertical fall.

It was utterly terrifying. Even as I write, the adrenalin flows again. And I relive the desperation of those last few seconds – before I blacked out.

I had no desire to talk to anyone as I entered the mess that night. The army detachment was stationed at our air base. They would be dining there too. I knew that my afternoon display of bravado might just as easily have killed them as well as me. I was convinced I would be severely disciplined, perhaps even court-martialled.

Very apprehensively, I watched as the army group entered the mess later in the evening. Almost immediately, their commander asked the question loudly. "Who is Para 35 with 75 Squadron?"

I squirmed uneasily behind my newspaper. One of the pilots gestured my way.

"Meyers, are you Para 35?" the army commander asked, making his way towards my table.

"Yes, sir," I replied, putting down my paper and standing to attention. He approached my chair. I stammered. "I know what you're going to say, sir. And I – "

He motioned me with his hand to stop talking. "Son," he interrupted, "I've been in this army for many years. I've seen operations in two wars. I've called down air support in live situations on many occasions. But never in all my experience have I seen a display of precision flying like you turned on for us today! That was incredible! Absolutely amazing."

I was flabbergasted. He estimated that my aircraft was five feet from the ground, below the level of the jeeps, as it roared by! And he thought it was brilliant!

But I knew it for what it was. An escape from death by a matter of inches. I can only imagine what the soldiers would have thought had they known that this daring and most impressive display of airmanship was being carried out by a completely unconscious pilot.

After that experience my flying became somewhat more measured and, hopefully, mature. I thought about it for many, many weeks. "What if?" questions kept coming back. What if I had delayed that pull-out one more microsecond?

Would God have moved Planet Earth just that little bit off its prescribed orbit to preserve my life? Of course not. We each are charged with the responsibility to manage our own lives, to live in a disciplined way within the parameters of maturity and common sense. And I went very close to throwing my life away.

And as I think about it today, I would never have known

Jo. Our five wonderful sons would never have been born. I would not have done what I have been privileged to do. My life would have been nothing more than a dim family memory by this time.

God is undoubtedly trustworthy. We can trust Him for anything. He will always do His part and fulfil His promises. But we, too, are a part of the equation of life. We have a part to play. Each choice we make has its own result. It is not God whose trust is to be doubted. It is in the responsibility we have for our lives, in the choices we make, that the challenge lies.

The Bible records some excellent advice that Paul gave to his protégé Timothy. He said,

> *"Timothy, guard what has been entrusted to your care."*
> 1 Timothy 6:20

Good advice!

3

Beauty from Ashes

Many are the plans in a man's heart, but it is the LORD's purpose that prevails.

Proverbs 19:21

"For I know the plans I have for you," declares the LORD, "plans to prosper you and not to harm you, plans to give you hope and a future."

Jeremiah 29:11

She stood below my window, a duffel bag slung provocatively over her shoulder. "Don't you want to come with me?" she said.

I envied the lifestyle of my friends with whom I worked, and flew, every day. They were wonderful guys. I loved being with them. But they enjoyed a certain freedom that I could not experience. Not as a Christian. They could do what they liked! None of them was bound by Christian criteria of behaviour. None of them had made any sort of Christian commitment. And they seemed to me to have such a great time. No restrictions. And so often, all they wanted was to include me in what they thought was fun. They didn't press. They simply offered. "Come on, man, come with us this weekend," they would say. "There'll be plenty of fun. Plenty of booze. Plenty of sex." They thought they could help me enjoy life more.

It was Friday. The girl who now stood outside my window was exceptionally pretty, with a great figure and a vivacious personality. She worked as a secretary in the airbase office. My thoughts were often filled with fantasies of being with her. To my amazement, a few days before, this very girl had invited me to go away with her for the weekend. I didn't think she even knew who I was. "We're all going," she said, "all your friends, and a whole lot of girls. Why don't you come with me? We'd have a lot of fun. It'll be a wild weekend!"

I was proud of the career choice I had made. It was the fulfilment of my boyhood ambition, my driving passion. But this was a different kind of choice. It was tough. It wasn't a career choice, and yet it was absolutely crucial. It was about lifestyle. Character. Faithfulness. Discipline. It was about sex and moral integrity. And the outcome of my decision would have a profound effect on my life.

Now, I had to choose. The thought of being with this girl had consumed my days and haunted my nights. I felt distracted, confused and very vulnerable. In my mind I argued for a compromise. I could at least experiment! Maybe I could give this attractive and tempting lifestyle a try for a while, enjoy it, and then turn my back on it! My family and Christian friends at home would never know! My world was far removed from theirs. In every way. It would be so easy. So new. So much fun.

But God would know. And I would know. So the battle raged on. And I prayed. I didn't know what else to do.

They were all getting ready to leave, and here she was, standing, waiting, invitingly. "Please come," she said again, with a dazzling, alluring smile.

How could I possibly say, "No, I don't want to,"? What a liar I would be. I had to decide. I had to choose.

It was a pivotal moment. I braced myself.

"I'm sorry. I just can't come." I said.

Almost immediately the battle that had raged within me all week was over. Minutes later, as she and my squadron friends drove off, I could hardly believe that I had somehow found the guts to say no. I greatly envied them the weekend that lay before them. And yet, at the same time, I knew that I had made a good decision. The right decision. I knew that had I gone with her it would have impacted my life profoundly. I knew I would have been irrevocably changed. I would have tarnished the standards I cherished and, I believe, jeopardised my future direction.

The pressure was gone. I felt a touch of approval, a godly hand of encouragement on my shoulder, as if a heavenly messenger was saying to me, "Okay, boy, that's over. The Father says you've done well. He'll have someone special for you later. You wait and see." And I thanked God for the courage He had given me.

Such choices are tough. They require a degree of strength that is often beyond us.

But He does give the strength, even in times of inordinate weakness, to make the right choice.

Not a pilot in the squadron was older than twenty-five. Our commanding officer, a major in the United States Air Force, was on exchange duty with the Royal Australian Air Force. He was a great guy. But then, he could afford to be. There was no war going on.

The Meteor fighters we flew were relatively old. The F86 Avon Sabre was the attention-getter, the first RAAF aircraft capable of supersonic flight. Our squadron was slated for re-equipment with these top-notch aircraft, but until that happened we weren't really in the public eye. Our more senior pilots were working on a Sabre conversion course that left us, the newer and younger pilots, somewhat to ourselves. This only meant one thing: exhilarating, extravagant fun!

It was playtime! Especially Friday mornings.

It was little more than a modern-day 'flying circus'. Unauthorised, but sanctioned! It took place every Friday morning at 0900 hours! There were four fighter units on our base. Two would be assigned to attack the base and two to defend it. Soon after 0800, as many as nine fighters – Meteors, Vampires and Sabres – would depart and take their positions. They alone knew where, but some twenty to thirty minutes later, they were ready to attack. Shortly after the first wave, another similar brace of fighters would take off in time to defend. Then, without warning, it would be on.

The ensuing mêlée over the base, with aircraft chasing each other, rolling and turning, looping and diving, high and low, was something to behold. A glorious airborne fracas.

"Red Four, look out, there's a Sabre on your tail! . . . Blue section, break right, break now, now!" The air waves were filled with excited, pumped-up young voices. "This one's mine! . . . Gotcha! . . . There's a twosome, three o'clock high! . . . Blue Three, is he still there? . . . You've gone, man, you've gone, you're finished! . . . Where the heck did he go? . . . I'm on minimum fuel . . . I'm out of here!"

It was the chatter of battle. Playing for fun, but training for keeps!

For the ground crew, it was Friday morning entertainment!

Finally we would all land, wet with sweat and low on fuel. We had all pulled so much 'G' trying with all our combined skill to shoot each other down and to avoid ploughing into some unsuspecting farmer's field, we were totally exhausted. There was no live ammunition, of course, but an hour or two later when the camera gun film was shown, there were 'winners and losers' nonetheless. And 'kills' were proudly recorded.

Who would ever walk away from a job like that?

In 1957 – at twenty-two years of age – I did.

Our squadron had been informed that when the re-equipment with Sabres was complete and we were proficient, we were to be moved to Malaya. Our new assignment was an active role in combating terrorist activity. Fooling around would be over.

There was only very scant news of terrorist incursion in Malaya. It certainly did not constitute an international threat. I recall asking a member of a bomber crew who had been in the region, "What do you attack?" He seemed to have no clear idea. It was just a matter of bombing assigned villages or jungle encampments. Another pilot said, "We try not to think about who gets killed. But as sure as night follows day, people do get killed."

Instead of being excited, as were all my fellow pilots, I began to feel a measure of disquiet. I knew I wasn't a fighter pilot just to have fun. I was not a pacifist. But the thought of being personally involved in indiscriminate bombing in peacetime, as a Christian, really began to disturb me. These feelings of discomfort grew and grew as the weeks went by. For the first time in my Air Force career I was not performing well. RAAF life began to take on a different meaning, and fighter flying lost some of its glamour. Was the door beginning to close on this chapter of my life?

And so it was with a strange mix of confidence and appre-hension that I approached my commanding officer to do the unthinkable for a fighter pilot – request a change of assign-ment. My American CO quickly referred it on to the base commander. It was a serious matter and soon became the topic of conversation in the crew room. When the time came for me to see the base commander, I was embarrassed and nervous. I had never had a one-on-one meeting with an officer of his rank!

"What's all this about, Meyers?" he began. He listened as I struggled to explain. I endeavoured to be very upfront about my position as a Christian. I was not trying in any way to be disloyal, nor was I refusing to accept an assignment. I was simply responding to deep apprehension about the task ahead. I told him about my long-term goals, my firmly held sense of calling to mission flying. I shared with him the distressing realisation that I might be killing exactly the kind of people I would be serving in the years to come. To my great surprise, he was very understanding, even sympathetic.

"You've done well here, Meyers," he said. "I really respect you and admire your convictions." We talked for about an hour. Finally, he said, "I will recommend that you be transferred to the Transport Wing, to the section currently in the USA being trained to fly the new C-130."

I was going to fly the Hercules. Another wonderful aircraft. I was wrong.

When my reassignment papers came, I was shocked. There was no posting to the Transport Wing, no assignment to fly the C-130 – or any other aircraft. Instead, my posting was to Adelaide, to non-flying administrative duties.

That was the 'bottom of the pack'! I could hardly believe it as I read my orders. A non-flying job! Grounded! Administrative duties! The Air Training Corps. Oh, God! Not that.

I found myself second-guessing my decision. Had I known this would happen, I would never have sought reassignment. I would have gladly stayed on as a fighter pilot. But to have my flying career cut off – was more than I could bear.

And I was deeply embarrassed in front of my fellow pilots.

Grounded! I just couldn't believe it. I felt like curling up into a little ball and crying myself to sleep that night. I felt discarded, let down by the Air Force – and by God.

In the weeks before I left, every day, I would see them. Those wonderful aircraft, in precise lines, sleek and grey. I would feel their engines crackle as my friends took off, two or four at a time. *That's my life going on out there*, I would think to myself. *The fulfilment of my childhood ambition. That's what I have been so good at doing . . . and I have spoiled it, ruined it.* My fighter career was over. The guys I had worked with, my best friends, considered me a fool. And there was no one else to blame but myself.

Dark days.

The squadron eventually went off to Malaya with their magnificent F-86s. I went to Adelaide, with my briefcase full of administrative papers, dejected, broken-hearted.

"Where is God in all this?" I asked. "I did this for Him, because I believed He wanted me to. And look at the result!"

But the pain was to worsen. I was to be accommodated at the Edinburgh Air Force Base about twenty miles north of Adelaide, where the operational unit for the multinational Weapons Research Establishment was located. From Edinburgh, highly classified and exciting test and development flying was carried out. I would be living with the men who did that flying, but every day I would have to drive twenty miles into the city – to work in an office.

Over and over again, in desperation, I cried out to God. I wondered whether He really knew what was happening. I doubt that any new appointee to a job has ever felt as negative as I did when I checked into my new responsibilities in Adelaide. I was assigned my office and sat there looking at all the 'stuff' of administration – filing cabinets, typewriters, foot-high heaps of files, and orders posted on the walls. I was devastated.

Could anything be more in stark contrast to the Friday morning dogfight at my old fighter base?

There was one small consolation. The pastor from my old church in Sydney was in Adelaide now. I desperately needed a listening and sympathetic ear, a shoulder to cry on. He would understand my misery and could comfort me in my despair. At least I could go to him.

Thus, on that first afternoon, as soon as I could get away, I went to see him. It had been some years since we had met.

"What on earth are you doing here?" Alan Tinsley asked joyfully, surprised as he opened the door. "I heard you were going to Malaya." He and his wife were just the same as I remembered them; she, beautiful and elegant, warm and welcoming; he, a large, outgoing man with a soft heart and a firm handshake.

I told him everything. It all poured out. My feelings of misgivings about Malaya, right through to my arrival in Adelaide earlier that day. He listened well. He always did. But his response was not at all what I expected. I had come for comfort, consolation and sympathy. But as my tale of woe came to an end, he looked me right in the eyes and said, "Who do you think you are? I never thought I'd see you in such a miserable state of mind, filled with self-pity. You're streets away from trusting God, Max!"

And over the next hour he delivered tough love to me. "Where is your trust in God?" he asked. "Do you think He doesn't know all about this? Do you think He has been frustrated by the Air Force in His plans for you? Come on, boy. Lift your backside off the ground and walk tall again. God knows exactly what He is doing with you. He is in complete control. Wake up to yourself – and address this thing as it really needs to be addressed."

After he had prayed for me, he said, "Now, let's go and have dinner. Joy will have something special for us. Then

I'm going to send you around to the church where the choir will be rehearsing. You can sing some of your woes away!"

Sing? That was the last thing I felt like doing. *No way,* I thought.

But Alan Tinsley, my friend and mentor, was a strong man. He wasn't fooling. Dinner over, Joy left for the choir practice while Alan and I chatted for a while. Then, as promised, he packed me off to the church, much against my will. It took me only a few minutes to walk the short distance, and as I entered through the vestibule I could hear the strains of a familiar anthem. Opening the door and feeling rather embarrassed, dressed as I was in my Air Force uniform, I walked right down the long aisle. The choir members, sitting in the angled seats under the pulpit, watched me all the way. I told the choir master that the pastor had said I was to sing in the tenor section of his choir!

It all seemed incongruous. Yes, I had always loved to sing – but not tonight! When I took my place with the tenors, I felt like crying, not singing! What a day it had been. What an emotional roller coaster.

As we practised familiar old anthems, however, I slowly began to feel better. A therapeutic work was being done in my heart. It was as if the arms of God were folding me to Himself. The words and music we were singing were soothing my troubled soul.

I also knew that Alan Tinsley, in his home around the corner, was praying for me. His words of tough love had hurt. But Alan and Joy had always loved me like the son they never had. And the truth of what he said had broken through the gloom of my anguish.

Standing in the tenor row of the choir stalls I began glancing around. These people were strangers to me. And as I looked down into the ranks in front of me, seeing only the backs of the sopranos, my attention was drawn to a girl standing beside Joy. A mass of curly blond hair spilled over the shoulders of a blue dress. A very nicely put together, athletic body with shapely legs and ankles that really captured my attention. My misery receded further still.

Come on, I chastised myself. *This is a house of God.* But I guess boys will be boys! And I thought, as I looked down during a pause in the practice, *The back looks really great. I wonder what the front side is like?* Then between anthems, as the next piece of music was being distributed, she turned around.

She looked at me. And I loved her. It was as simple as that. I didn't know her name. And I certainly knew nothing about her. All I knew was that she was the most exciting, spectacular girl I had ever seen in my life. Suddenly I was glad I was there. Not anywhere else. Not even getting ready to go to Malaya.

I think there was a twinkle in God's eye as He looked down on me.

After choir practice was over, people chatted and introduced themselves to me. They were so friendly, so welcoming. But I could not keep my eyes off the girl in the blue dress. The memory of her standing there by the organ on the red carpet, talking with Joy Tinsley, is one I shall never forget. Then Joy turned to me and said, "Max, I want you to meet a friend of ours, Jo Lawton." A pair of blue eyes looked into mine. "Hi, it's great to have you here. You have a really nice voice. I could hear you singing behind me." I know we talked for a few minutes, but I am sure I was utterly incoherent.

Walking out to the parking area shortly afterwards, I was in a daze. And to my absolute delight, Alan, who had offered to drive me back to the Air Force base, called out to this captivating curly-headed girl, now standing with someone else, "Hey Jo, come for a ride! Joy and I are going to take this guy back to the RAAF base at Edinburgh. Come on. We'll drop you home later."

I was incredulous. Intrigued. In love. And I was going to ride with her in the Tinsleys' car all the way back to the base. My misery had vanished.

I learned that this Jo Lawton was a gifted musician. For most of her twenty-three years she had played the piano. Having studied with one of Australia's great teachers and graduated from the Elder Conservatorium of Music, she was now a high-school teacher of music as well as physical education. A fine organist. A choir director. I wasn't to learn until much later that her own dream, her own driving passion, had always been to become a missionary doctor one day.

At first I thought that she had been placed in my path as a further test of my commitment to serve in mission. There was no way I could imagine this girl, from such a cultured background, living in the jungle where I was planning to spend my future. But she would. She was designed for me. An incredibly intelligent, exquisite love gift from God, she had been chosen to be my life's partner and would love me, walk with me, fly with me. She would bring to my life a great measure of richness and sophistication, enhancing and encouraging in me the development of so many qualities I would need in future years. And while I wasn't to know until much later, this Jo *was* mine. That curly-headed blonde from the soprano line eventually became my wife and the mother of our five boys, Michael, Timothy, Jonathon, Robin and Christopher.

I didn't know, as we climbed into the back of the car that memorable night, that she would eventually leave her world, put aside her own dreams, to join mine. All I knew was that I had fallen hopelessly in love. Some months later, to my profound joy and great surprise, I found that she had fallen in love with me at the same time.

A chance meeting? Love at first sight? Or a miracle in the hand of God – a master stroke on the canvas of our lives.

From the soprano line in the church choir that night, Jo began a flight with me that has enhanced my own flight. She has brought immeasurable strength and power to me and to many others as well along the way. She has been used in the lives of many people who serve all over the world today.

For me, this life of ours has been relatively easy. I grew up wanting to fly. That dream became my calling in teenage years, my reality as an adult. I've been involved in aviation for almost all of my working life. But for Jo it has been different. She didn't grow up with a passion for aeroplanes. She was highly successful in a totally different arena. Then, at twenty-three, I came into her life and it took a completely different direction. There was to be no more playing with symphony orchestras or conducting beautiful choirs. No concerts to go to, no record player, not even a piano for a long time. Hardest of all, no dreams of a new career in medicine.

It has been a profound sacrifice.

I could have gone to Malaya. I certainly didn't choose to go to Adelaide. I hated the very thought of that assignment and felt dragged there like a resisting puppy. But I was being led by a Master who, although I didn't understand it, knew what was best for me and wanted me to have it.

And I have found Him to be totally and completely trust-worthy. It was His plan, implemented through others, that brought Jo and me together.

We were married by Alan Tinsley. We walked out of the church under the shiny crossed swords of an Air Force honour guard. Alan and Joy stood in the background, smiling.

Eventually I was assigned, as a pilot again, to Edinburgh Air Force Base, that place of so much sadness on the day of my arrival in Adelaide. The flying experience I received there in the next two years was beyond imagining in its value, far surpassing what it would have been had I remained a fighter pilot. I flew seven different types of aircraft – twin- and four-engined bombers as well as fighter and transport aircraft, even the huge Vickers Valiant, one of the three British V-Bombers. All of this was in a weapons research and development mode. In my final year I flew an aircraft for America's NASA, working to train Project Mercury tracking crews. This was an added bonus in what proved to be the best technical preparation I could possibly have had for service with MAF. A wonderful gift from God.

But God's most precious gift to me came from the soprano line in the church choir that night.

4

Doubts

*My son, do not forget my teaching, but keep my commands
in your heart, . . . Trust in the LORD with all your heart
and lean not on your own understanding; in all your ways
acknowledge him, and he will make your paths straight.*

Proverbs 3:1, 5–6

Sometimes we doubt.

It might have been only yesterday when the presence of
God seemed so very real. More real, perhaps, than things
that were visible. Yet today, from the deep recesses of the
mind, something emerges that makes us wonder – and
question. The basis of our faith doesn't feel quite as solid as
it did before. "What if . . . ?" we ask. Having no ready answers
we begin to doubt. And we feel so bad.

It might be an unresolved problem from years ago that
should have been long since dealt with. It might be a recurring
fear about the future. It might be a flawed relationship that
threatens our faith. Our prayers go unanswered. It seems
that absolutely nothing can be done about it, and from the
depths of our being comes the cry, "Where is God? Where,
really, is He?"

It has happened to me on more than one occasion. One of
these times was many years ago, when I was still in the military.

I was a proud, young Australian Air Force pilot. My work was exciting, so exciting, in fact, that it didn't feel like work at all. Number 2 Air Trials Unit, based north of Adelaide, South Australia, was a strategic part of an international missile and weapons development strategy. We were embroiled in the cold war. Much of my flying was classified as top secret. I was flying seven types of aircraft. Most pilots specialise on one type. No other unit offered anything like this. In the morning I might fly a twin-jet British-built Canberra bomber, testing some aspect of the development of a top-secret missile. In the afternoon I could find myself at the controls of a highly modified fighter, preparing it for its 'target' role in the ground-to-air missile development programme. The next day it might be a bomb ballistics trial in a Vickers Valiant V-Bomber.

In the summer of 1960 we entered the Space Race. I was assigned to work with NASA's Project Mercury. My responsibility was to fly a C-47 'Dakota', specially configured as a test platform to train NASA's tracking crews. My aircraft carried a complete duplicate of the Mercury capsule's instrumentation. Using highly advanced telemetry we could simulate, over Australia's vast, red outback, the passage of a space capsule in orbit.

This was military flying at its best. It could have been said of us, "They have the right stuff."

Many years before, as a teenager, I had promised God that if I were to become a professional pilot I would dedicate my skills and abilities to mission flying whenever and wherever He wanted me to serve. The sense of responsibility to that promise had never left me. Yes, I had a great job. I loved the planes I was flying. I loved the people I was working with. It was the fulfilment of my boyhood ambition . . . my dream. But it was only to be for a brief period. I knew that. I had signed on for six years of service and had completed seven.

There was always another sort of flying awaiting me . . . somewhere. And so it was with a sense of joyful anticipation that at the peak of my military flying career I submitted the resignation of my Air Force commission.

I will never forget the day in April 1961 when the response arrived. My resignation had been accepted. I would be released from military service on June 30. By this time I had made application and had been accepted by MAF for service as a pilot in Papua New Guinea, conditional upon my release from the Air Force. There was no doubt in my mind that great things were ahead. And yet there was a genuine sadness at the prospect of moving out of my familiar and very much-loved world. It was also somewhat threatening to be leaving the financial security of military life, and abandoning a wonderful career, to launch into something about which I really knew so little.

But I had made a commitment. There was no going back. My Air Force career was over. I had burned the bridges behind me.

It was then I began to doubt.

What have you done? I asked myself. *What if it doesn't work out with MAF? What have you got then?* My faith wavered.

Of course it would be okay . . . wouldn't it?

I had been working towards this point for ten years.

Of course God was trustworthy. I had experienced that over and over again. But was He really? Could He be trusted with something as momentous as this?

And as weeks went by, a voice of doubt taunted me, gnawing away at the very basis of my faith.

I became overwhelmed. As the date of release from the Air Force drew nearer, the work I was doing became all the more fascinating and attractive. I became more and more convinced I was a fool to walk away from such opportunity.

My doubt was not restricted to questions about career. It

grew deeper. I had always expected that my departure from military life would be like a wonderful graduation. I thought that these would be great days of confidence in God, of joyful assurance that I was walking the right path. Instead I found myself wondering where God was and why He didn't deal directly with my troubled heart and fill me with confident trust. I found myself wondering if I was even right to believe in a 'personal call' and if God really did have a plan for my life.

I wondered if He was real at all!

Did it really matter what I did with my life? I was a pilot. Would I not have been much better off to depend on my own ability and take control of my own career?

I told no one of these doubts. I couldn't. I didn't tell my wife. I couldn't tell my Air Force colleagues. My friends at church were even harder to tell. I certainly couldn't tell the MAF people. So I wallowed in my doubts – alone.

MAF had requested that I come to Melbourne for further interviews and orientation. I was very apprehensive about it. Could I hide my doubts from them? Would they see through me? What would they say, or do, if they knew how totally confused I was? Career-wise, MAF was now my only option. If I failed in this, where would I be?

Previously I had used an Air Force jet fighter to go to Melbourne. We were required to do a certain amount of 'continuation training', and a trip to Melbourne was easily justified as a navigational exercise. This time, though, I decided to drive the four hundred and fifty miles and stay for the weekend. On Sunday, grasping in my own darkness for a solution to the agonising dilemma that was taking place within me, I decided to attend a large Melbourne church where a great friend was the pastor. He had been so helpful to me in the past. Perhaps he might have something to say that would rescue me from my terrible despair. I prayed, in the desperation of my doubt, that in his sermons of that weekend there would be a message of reassurance for me.

There was no enlightening message from my pastor friend, no revelation to dispel my gloom. Of course, I was too embarrassed to share my dilemma with him.

I found myself on that Sunday night almost at the end of my ability to cope. I didn't want to talk with anyone. I didn't want to stay in Melbourne. In a very real sense I didn't want to go home either. I was a mess. John Bunyan described my situation so aptly as the 'Slough of Despond'.

Rather than go back to where I had been staying, I decided to get on the road and drive through the night home to Adelaide.

Having set out soon after the evening church service, I found myself, a couple of hours later, approaching the regional city of Ballarat. Alone in the car, I had cried out repeatedly to the One whom by this time I was almost convinced was a totally disinterested and non-hearing God. With deep emotion, I prayed, "God, what am I going to do? Please help me . . . if you are there. I can't go on like this."

There was no answer.

At the western end of Ballarat there is a memorial arch across the highway, a kind of mini 'Arc de Triumph'. I had passed under this arch many times.

As I approached, travelling at about sixty miles per hour, I noticed a man sitting at its base in the darkness. He stood to his feet and cocked his thumb at me. It was awfully late, about midnight, so I knew he really needed a ride.

I saw the plea in his face as I sped past. *Not tonight*, I thought. *I don't care how desperate you are. I don't want to talk with anyone.* If I had stopped, I could not have hidden from him the emotional upheaval that was taking place in my life. I didn't want to explain this to anyone, let alone a man trying to thumb a lift.

So I drove on.

It must have been thirty minutes later, and at least thirty or forty miles farther along the road, that I began to think a little differently. *Has God ever left me? Was it possible that the voices of doubt, self-pity and shame were shouting so loudly in my ears that I could not hear what God was saying?*

I had to acknowledge that was not only possible but likely.

Then the thought came to me. Although God hadn't used my friend the pastor to speak to me, there may be others. Suddenly I remembered the stranger standing by the arch. Maybe he was there, just for me.

No, that's a ludicrous idea. It's illogical. Ridiculous.

I drove on for a while thinking about him. Who was he? What would he have said to me had I stopped and picked him up? What would I have said to him? No, it was stupid to think that he could be a messenger to me. But slowly the conviction grew in my mind that this man could be of significance to me, that he could have been placed there by God, just for me, at this very moment.

No one saw me stop the car, turn around on the highway, and make my way back towards Ballarat. It was a crazy thing to do. The hitch-hiker would, in all probability, be long since gone. But I drove all that way back. I had to do it.

And he was still there.

This time, of course, I was approaching from the opposite direction so he didn't even stand up. He didn't need a ride in the direction my car was heading. I drove through the arch, turned around, rolled down the window, and stopped by him.

"Want a lift?" I asked him.

I guess he couldn't understand why a car should appear out of the darkness from the west, turn around in front of him, and offer him a ride back in a westerly direction. His wariness was apparent. "No, thanks. I'm wanting to go back there where you've come from."

"Well, mate, that's where I'm going now. Come on, hop in. I'll take you home."

We didn't say a word to each other for some time as I drove towards Adelaide. I'm sure he was wondering exactly what was happening. I didn't want to talk with him anyway. I just wanted to know if he had something to say – from God!

As I watched him out of the corner of my eye, he sat quietly staring at the dashboard of the car. After a while I noticed a change in his demeanour. He was breathing deeply. I sensed tension, confusion. He sighed a loud sigh, a couple of times, as if something was really bothering him. Then, with a voice filled with emotion, he said to me, "Mate, we haven't talked yet, but I simply have to ask you something. I don't know who you are or why you picked me up. Seems to me you were going the other way. I don't know if you can understand my question, let alone answer it, but I need to ask you something. It's terribly important to me just now."

I didn't want questions from him. I wanted answers! But I told him to go ahead anyway.

"It may seem like a crazy question," he said, "but it's simply this." He hesitated. "Do you believe in God? I have to know."

I was totally startled by what he had said. Who on earth was this man? Driving back to the arch was more an act of desperation on my part than anything else. I was the needy one. From the emptiness of my store of faith I had nothing to offer him. After all, I was the one who stood in need of spiritual help and counsel. How could I, of all people, confirm the reality and presence of God to some stranger, and a hitch-hiker at that?

Evasively I said, "Why do you ask a question like that?"

"I'll have to tell you a story," he said. "It'll probably sound ridiculous, but I have to tell you.

"On Saturday I went by train to Melbourne to watch football," he said. "I met some friends there and after the game we went for a quick drink, but it turned out to be anything but quick. My friends and I drank long into the evening, well after the departure time of my train back home. I had no other option but to spend the night there. There's only one train a day on our line at the weekend. So this afternoon I went to the station in plenty of time to catch the Sunday train. And an amazing thing happened there.

"A bloke stood on the footpath preaching. I'm a country boy from Horsham, and street preachers would be a bit of a joke there. But something made me want to listen to him. He described my life exactly. Hopeless. Not a lot of direction. He spoke about God . . . and love. He said that God was the answer to my problems. He told me I could know God like a father. He used the word 'lost' . . . exactly how I felt.

"It was time for the train," he continued, "but I couldn't walk away from this man. I had to listen, so I let the train go. What he was talking about was more important than going home."

As my passenger went on with his story, he explained that he had never heard anything like this before. After the street preacher had finished, he had spoken with him personally, asking whether such an amazing story applied to him. And this time, face to face, he heard again the story of God's love, of forgiveness and . . . eternal life. He heard of a saviour who died and rose again to draw even football fans to Himself.

"I found myself, right there in the street with everybody around, repeating a prayer, the very first prayer of my life. I asked God to forgive me. I asked Him to give me that new life I had just heard about," he told me.

"This preacher bloke took me to meet his friends at a church, and speaking with them, I knew that something marvellous had happened to me. I came to Melbourne to watch a footy match and I had found God. Actually, God had found me. Mate, I have never felt anything like the feelings I had there.

"But I had to get home," he said. "I have to be at work in the morning. The people from the church drove me a number of miles out of town to thumb a ride home. It was quite a while before anyone stopped for me. I got as far as Ballarat a couple of hours ago. I've been sitting under that arch for ages trying to get another ride.

"I gotta admit. Last night was amazing, but sitting there alone in the cold has been a bad, bad time. I've been turning over in my mind all that happened in Melbourne.

"But then I began to doubt.

"What really had happened? Could my life have been so totally changed through hearing a story and praying a prayer? Who were those people? How do I know it's true? None of my family or friends believe this stuff. How am I going to tell them? Have I been hoodwinked or brainwashed by some religious nut?

"So, I've been sitting at the base of that arch arguing with myself and asking God to show Himself to me. I'd almost decided to forget the whole thing. Maybe it was something weird that had happened and that should be forgotten. But I couldn't do it. It had been too real."

He went on with his incredible story as the miles passed by.

"Finally," he said, "just before you came, in desperation I stood and cried out to God the second prayer of my life. If you are real, God, please send someone to tell me. Please. Please."

He looked across at me, pleading. "So, do you think this is all crazy, or not? Whether you can answer my question or not, I have to ask it. Do you believe in God?"

Did I believe in God? This newborn believer, fresh in the knowledge of a salvation that was real but already under threat, was asking me to confirm the validity of his actions in Melbourne the previous evening. As his story unfolded, I had heard the voice of God speaking to me, answering the cries of my own soul, filling me with a new certainty of faith. This was a divine appointment – for me! I was totally reassured. My reassured heart said to me, "Go on, you tell him. Tell him that God is real. Tell him that God is utterly and completely trustworthy."

And so I did.

"You've told me your story," I then said to him. "Now I have to tell you mine. Yes, God is trustworthy. God is real. Even in the times of heart-wrenching doubts. In fact, He is here in this car. Right now. My doubts, your doubts, don't change Him at all. And I've been brought here to tell you just that. He does love you. He is love. And last night He gave to you the honour of knowing Him personally."

I went on to share with him my own terrible time of doubting. I told him of my need for someone to come into my life and bring me God's message of assurance. I told him that I believed he was that person. God had sent him to me . . .

A great and wonderful encounter took place in the middle of that cold Australian night in a yellow Holden car. The Creator of the universe poured out blessing into that car upon two very needy young men. He took a brand-new baby-believer and through him lifted me out of the depth of my misery and despond, never to doubt His reality again. And He took me, in my wretched state of personal need, and through me lifted a new but wavering child-in-the-faith, to nurture him and set his feet on the right path.

It blows my mind to think of God working so intricately and beautifully with His children. He tells us that He is a shepherd, tenderly caring for His flock, giving special attention to the newborn and to those who wander away.

I thought I could unravel the tangled mess of my life

myself. I wanted to be alone that night in my car, wallowing in confusion and misery. But God had a better way. He knew that what I really needed was to be reminded that He, God, remains essentially relational. He works through people. Even the youngest of His children.

And He never stops loving us, even when we doubt Him the most.

PART 2

5

Why?

*"I will speak out in the anguish of my spirit, I will complain
in the bitterness of my soul . . . I prefer strangling and
death, rather than this body of mine. I despise my life;
I would not live for ever. Let me alone; my days have no
meaning."*

Job 7:11, 15–16

"Oh God, please. Make her stop."

My prayer was born out of startled shock as I stood with a
group of men encircling the bent-over, bloodstained figure
of a Papua New Guinean woman.

But God didn't make her stop. And I couldn't.

As soon as I moved forward to intervene, my arms were
gripped by two of the men standing alongside me. Their
fingers bit deeply into my flesh. Their scowling faces and
words of unmistakable rebuke made it abundantly clear that
I was to do nothing. I wasn't wanted there. This was their
culture. They wanted me to leave.

The woman was killing herself, and I could do nothing
about it.

It was gruesome, abhorrent and shocking. The beliefs and
practices of these mountain people, the men restraining me,

demanded that I did not interfere. I did not understand this rare and violent clash of cultures. They were in control.

The place was a small airstrip at Lake Kopiago in the Western Highlands of Papua New Guinea. It was about noon on a clear bright day in 1965, and I had flown to Kopiago to deliver a load of freight to the mission staff there. Usually a small crowd stood around the parking bay when the plane arrived. This time there was no crowd. And the young national man from the mission who always came to meet me was nowhere to be seen. Something was wrong. He was always on time.

But he was there. As I shut down the engine, he appeared, running over to the plane from a short distance away where a group of about twenty men were gathered. Whatever was happening there, they were intently involved.

My friend was deeply disturbed and pulled me by the arm towards this group as soon as I stepped down from the plane. "Please come. Maybe you can help," he said as he hurried me over towards the group. "They won't let me do anything to stop her." He forced a way for me through the men to the centre of the circle.

I could hardly believe what I saw next.

A Kopiago lady was kneeling on the ground. Her head and body were covered in blood. It ran in rivulets down her face, congealing on her bare body, her thighs and her knees. Spattered blood covered the grey stony ground on which she knelt. In her bloodied hands she clutched a large, round river stone. She was beating her own head to a bloody pulp. Her forehead was completely split open.

The men stood around in silence, watching but not interfering.

Again she lifted the stone from between her knees with both hands and with what seemed superhuman force smashed it into her forehead. The stone fell to the ground, and her head dropped to her knees as she reeled in semi-conscious agony. Forcing herself back into consciousness a minute or so later she picked up the bloodied stone and did it again. Over and over she repeated the horrendous, self-inflicted hammering. I couldn't believe her strength and the force she was able to generate. I couldn't believe that she could survive what she was doing to herself. It was as if she were controlled by some external power.

Within minutes she lay face down on the blood-spattered rocks, unconscious again and, I thought, dying. I struggled to be free, to help her. But I was held fast by the men and was unable to move. After watching for a while, I finally pulled myself free and turned away with a sickened heart. I could do nothing.

The men were glad to see me go. They were angry with me for trying to interfere. I was angry with them for not allowing me to do so. They said very little. Only that the woman had lost a child earlier that morning. Her one remaining child. She had called upon the tribal spirits of the Kopiago people to save her child, but to no avail. She had previously lost her husband, and now all of her children. Grief and anguish drove her to this gruesome action. Life held no hope for her. It was not worth living.

A short while later, as I took off from Kopiago, I could see the small group of men still encircling that dreadful scene. Yet, the next time I landed there I was greeted with the usual friendly smiles. There was no mention of what had happened previously. It was something I knew I could never understand. It was an incident that had come and gone.

But Kopiago for me is always synonymous with pain. And deep, spiritual need.

Why bother with mission?

I face the question often these days.

In some circles these days the word *missionary* seems to

carry connotations of yesteryear. "Mission belongs to another generation," they say. Many times I have been asked why I have spent my life helping missionaries in cross-cultural situations. "You people in mission are overbearing and patronising. You will achieve nothing other than the destruction of wonderful tribal cultures."

I could take those people, with their criticisms, to remote and exotic places all over the world and show them what has been done in the name of Christian mission.

I could show them people whose culture remains intact. I could show them hospitals, medical facilities and flying doctor services that bring relief from the hopelessness of former days.

Mostly, I'd like to show them Kopiago. God has done a great work of grace among the people of the Lake Kopiago area since those early days of mission. Once, in an earlier time, suicide was the only answer to the agony of a lonely woman's quiet grief, and the hopelessness of life. In the lives of so many of them, despair has been replaced by hope! The people of Kopiago are now permeated by the knowledge, the powerful presence, and the real comfort of God who created them and loves them.

Why? Why interfere with these people? Why bother with missions? For me, the answer lies at the cross of Christ.

And amongst the stones of Kopiago.

6

Tough Decisions

If any of you lacks wisdom, he should ask God, who gives generously to all without finding fault, and it will be given to him. But when he asks, he must believe and not doubt.

James 1:5–6

Flying aeroplanes with safety always demands maturity in decision-making. Wise choices. Military flying, I had found, was usually under close direction. Following orders. But I was to learn that MAF flying brought with it an added dimension of responsibility, choices that were often mine, and mine alone, to make. And sometimes, those choices were tough.

One evening, at about 5:30, I landed at Telefomin, a government post and mission station close to Papua New Guinea's western border. We almost never flew into Telefomin after 2:00 in the afternoon. The mountain passes and valleys in the area were usually filled with cloud by then.

But this was a medical emergency. For these flights we tried a little bit harder. I knew lives were at stake that day.

The patient was neither a Papua New Guinea national, nor mission staff. She was the wife of the patrol officer and, seven months into her pregnancy, she had gone into early labour. There were complications, however. Telefomin's small clinic was not able to provide this woman the specialist care she needed.

I had asked the staff there to have her at the airstrip. "If she's ready, I can throw my cargo off and be airborne again in just a couple of minutes. We should be able to get her to Wewak a bit after last light." It was an inhospitable country even in the daytime, so night flights were not permitted. In those days Papua New Guinea aircraft were not fitted with the appropriate instrumentation for flying after dark.

But the patient wasn't ready. She hadn't even been brought to the airstrip. "She's still down at the clinic, and has taken a turn for the worse," I was told. "We just can't move her right now."

I looked up to see the lengthening shadows beginning to darken the Telefomin valley. "Then we'll just have to wait until morning," I said reluctantly. I hoped she would make it through the night. I climbed into the waiting jeep, and we drove down through the mission station to the clinic. The valley would be enshrouded in darkness by 6:30pm.

But right at 6:30 there was a knock on the door of the house where I was eating supper. It was the sister from the clinic, clearly agitated. "She's in deep trouble, Max. She's getting worse and needs care that I can't give her. I don't think she'll last through the night. I've been in touch with the doctors in Wewak, but we don't have the medication they say we need. Even if we can get her to Wewak it may still be touch and go. Is there anything you can do? Is there any way that you could fly her out – now?"

Flying the plane at night was not the problem. A great deal of my military flying had been done at night. But that was in very sophisticated aircraft, not single-engined Cessnas, and certainly not in Papua New Guinea's rugged terrain. The weather also concerned me. Conditions had been quite good as I had flown in from Wewak late in the afternoon, and the present 'overcast' at Telefomin was reasonably high. But I had absolutely no idea what had happened along the track through the mountains during the couple of hours since I had come that way. The weather always changed so quickly in those mountains.

I had enough fuel on the plane to cover more than the required daytime reserves. Wewak had been alerted to the possibility of an emergency night flight and was reporting that the weather was clear. But there was no report to cover the hundred or so miles through the mountains and over the western reaches of the Sepik Basin.

What should I do? It wasn't an easy choice. I prayed for wisdom and sound judgement. I decided to try. Before leaving I explained to the missionaries that I would need emergency lighting on the airstrip in the event that I were to find the weather impassable and elect to return. "If you hear me come back into the valley, drive one of the jeeps to each end of the airstrip. Park them just on the other side of the eastern boundary line and shine their lights towards each other. If you could also have a small fire lit at about the halfway mark on the same side of the strip, that would help."

What a place for a woman in labour, I thought as I laid her down on a thin mattress on the cold metal floor of my small Cessna. She knew only too well that planes like mine didn't fly around at night in that territory. Apprehension and fear must have compounded her pain and discomfort.

As I sat at the top end of that airstrip, my pre-take-off checks, as usual, included a quiet but particularly earnest prayer for guidance, for help, for wise judgement. The aircraft's landing light was adequate for take-off, but it was so dark, so very black as I climbed away towards the invisible range ahead. A turn to the right, however, allowed me to see the lights of the Telefomin station and to set a north-easterly course heading between the mountains. To climb to altitude above them would have placed my patient at even more risk.

There was no moon, but I could faintly make out the rough outline of towering ridges against the night sky on either side as I flew along in the darkness. Two shades of black. Once out of the high ranges, I saw below the occasional red glow of fire from scattered Sepik villages. While still many miles from the coast, the lights of the small town of Wewak became visible, dimly at first, then a patch of twinkling brightness against the dark mass of the sea. I had lived there for years, but this was the first time I had seen the 'lights of home' at night, from my aircraft.

The landing at the town's airport was uneventful. An ambulance was waiting, as was the obstetrician from the hospital.

As Jo and I drove home we talked quietly. Two lives had been saved.

A tough choice. A good decision. A good result.

It was Sunday morning at Wasua, a Papua New Guinean village on the banks of the mighty Fly River.

We loved our little bush home there. It was a classic mission house. Perched high on wooden stilts, its walls were of plaited bamboo. It had a thatched grass roof at the front. Over the rear of the house, galvanised iron caught the rainwater and funnelled it into the large tank by the back door. There was no electricity. A wood-burning stove was Jo's only cooking facility in that hot and humid environment.

Pioneer living.

Our toilet system was unique, to say the least. The 'deep hole/long drop' type, generic to most mission homes, would not work in this flood-prone area. One struck water only about six inches below the surface. Instead, we had a 'barely private' outdoor lean-to, containing a wooden seat positioned over a disgusting black bucket. Michael, the eldest of our five sons, now a lawyer in Australia, says he remembers as a three-year-old, that the huge spiders inhabiting the dense festoons of cobwebs in the gabled thatch of that outhouse roof were 'as big as my face'.

On the far side of the yard there was a large pit of sodden sawdust. In it, a veritable army of microbes and other 'beasties' waited for their weekly offering from that revolting bucket. It always amazed me how clean the sawdust looked when I dug into it for the next deposit! It was like a special disappearing trick! Those microbes were masters at sleight-of-hand.

Wasua really was a quaint place!

This particular morning, church was to commence in thirty minutes, and Jo was getting our three little guys ready. I walked down to the radio room to check that all was well in the network of mission stations spread over hundreds of miles from the North to the West. The people out there were 'my' people. My constituency. MAF was their flying life-link.

But at Suki, about eighty miles to the west of Wasua, there was a medical emergency. "It's a snake-bite case," the caller said. "We've identified the species of snake, but we have no antivenin for its poison. The man will die if we can't get him to the hospital at Daru quickly."

So much for church with my family that morning. As the congregation sat on the split-palm floor of the quaint little bush church, their harmonious Papua New Guinean singing was interrupted by the howl of the Cessna's engine as I took off along the grass airstrip about seventy-five yards away.

The flight was uneventful. The track was simple. West along the Fly River for thirty minutes, then straight ahead, paralleling another smaller river where the Fly turned up to the North. As I passed overhead, scores of crocodiles, sunning themselves on the muddy banks, slid with a splash into the water at the sound of the plane. It was a fun place to fly. No mountains here, just thousands of square miles of tropical forest and swamplands intersected by muddy rivers, all draining into the Fly.

Finally, there ahead was Suki, and the expected group of people waiting at the parking bay of the rough airstrip. I landed and taxied to where the patient was lying on a stretcher.

He was drifting in and out of consciousness. The poison of the snake was killing him, shutting down his respiratory system by filling it with fluid. Streams of foul, thick mucus ran from his nose and mouth. Flies swarmed around his mouth, nose and eyes. I almost retched.

In spite of his condition, he clutched firmly in his hand the head and about three inches of the body of the snake. The people knew that if they could send the offending reptile with the patient, the correct antivenin could be identified and used to neutralise the effect of the poison.

There was no time to be lost. It was a quick turnaround.

As I taxied the aircraft to the far end of the airstrip, I glanced at the patient lying on the floor beside me. He looked horrible. This ghastly stuff just seemed to keep pouring from him. The nurse at Suki had thoughtfully wrapped cloth around his neck and placed it under his head to save making a mess in the plane.

I thought he was going to die – in my plane – even before we were airborne.

I prayed before I took off. For him, for healing. For me to be used in that healing process. I wondered if he would be better sitting upright. Perhaps he would be more able to breathe in that position, I thought. But there was no seat for him. Anticipating a stretcher patient, all the passenger seats had been removed and left behind at Wasua. But he could at least sit on the floor propped up against the rear of the cabin.

So I stopped at the end of the airstrip, shut down the engine, and jumped out. I ran around the plane to the passenger door, climbed in and hoisted my semi-conscious passenger into a sitting position, then dragged him to the back. There was no seat strap there, so he sat unrestrained, leaning against the bulkhead. The same revolting mess continued to run down his chest.

Obviously wondering why I had done this, the Suki staff ran along the strip towards me. But I didn't have time to wait for them. This man was close to death. It would take an hour to get to Daru – and every second counted.

"What's up? Why did you shut down?" one of the men shouted as he ran up to the aircraft. "It's okay," I yelled, climbing back into the pilot's seat. "I just had to change the patient's position. I'm ready now. Stand clear. I really need to get going." And with a twist of the ignition key, the engine once again burst into life. I turned into the wind and took off.

Throughout the flight to Daru, moans, horrible spasmodic coughs and choking noises continued from behind me.

There was no means to communicate ahead my impending arrival at Daru. Such a small place didn't merit a control tower. But I had a procedure worked out with the medical officer there. If I had need of an ambulance I would gun the engine once, that is, close and open the throttle, as I flew over the hospital and his house. If there was some degree of emergency I would do so twice. For a really urgent emergency, three times.

I knew he would be in church at the time, so it was over the hospital, over the doctor's house, then low over the church. I gunned the engine four, five, six times. Every inhabitant of the tiny island town would know this was an emergency!

Normally, I could depend upon seeing the dust of the ambulance approaching along the road as I shut down the engine. This time, however, I waited and waited. And I prayed, "Lord God. Please. Save this man's life."

By now my passenger was unconscious. Hoping to save precious minutes and perhaps his life, I dragged him out of the plane and tried to sit him up on the grass against the plane's wheel. He tipped over sideways. So I propped him up again. Once more he toppled over. After one more fruitless attempt, I laid him down on the grass in the shade of the wing. "You'll just have to lie down there," I muttered to myself. He was oblivious to this strange sit-up-lie-down performance. Apart from occasional spasmodic gasps and that dreadful choking sound, he was barely breathing. I could do no more for him. Time went by. I expected him to die at any moment.

But he held fast to the snake's head.

I was thinking about getting airborne again to fly once more over the town just as the doctor arrived. Then an ambulance. "Man, I'm sorry we're late," he said as his driver backed the ambulance up to where the patient was lying. "My team must have been all over the island. What have you got for us this time?"

"Look in his hand," I said.

He leaned down and prised the snake from the patient's firm grip. "That's an unusual one. It's very poisonous," he said. "It's a rare, 'small-eyed' snake. Look." He turned the snake over. It didn't seem to have any eyes at all.

"We do have the right stuff for him," he said confidently. "I think we can save him."

The ambulance raced off with the patient on board.

I walked with the doctor to his car.

"I don't know how it is that you MAF guys seem to know so much about medical things," he said casually. "So much about everything, it seems. It's amazing. I mean, how did you know to lay that fellow down flat like you did? Instead of sitting him up."

I shifted uneasily. "Huh?" I said.

"Laying him down in the plane and on the ground here probably saved his life," he said. "Do you know what, Max? If he'd been sitting up, he would have died!"

I said nothing.

As I took off later, I thought about the ghastly coughing and choking noises. Between the snake and I, that poor man just about used up every chance he had.

The next week I flew him back to Suki, totally recovered. He sat up all the way. Again.

A bad decision. A good result.

I was pushing the weather in the late afternoon, trying to get back to Wapenamanda, my highland base. Having already been away for three days doing maintenance on the aircraft, I tried just a little bit harder. Nights away weren't the favourite part of MAF life for Jo and me. It was much later than I would normally choose to do this flight, but at least it was worth the try.

As I approached the Central Range climbing through thirteen thousand feet to get above the rapidly rising clouds, Jo called on the radio to tell me that there was a medical situation at Kandep, about twenty minutes' flying from Wapenamanda. "They're asking that you uplift a pregnant European missionary to the hospital here. It's really urgent. She's some weeks early but has gone into labour," Jo said. "They've got to get her out of there."

Not another one of these, I thought. *Just like Telefomin.* But unlike that situation some time earlier, the weather on this day was ominous and getting worse. I couldn't see how I could even get to Kandep, let alone pick up a patient and fly her back to Wapenamanda. A wall of blackening cloud and a massive range of mountains blocked the path.

However, with difficulty and by diverting a few miles, I was able to descend into the western side of the Kandep valley some thirty minutes later and carefully make my way under the low, threatening cloud to the airstrip.

A mission nurse was waiting for me. "I think we'll have to call it off, Max," she said. "She's in the final stage of labour, and she simply doesn't want to fight weather like this in your plane. She's had a normal pregnancy thus far and, as a nurse herself, feels that the baby will be okay. Maybe she's right."

I decided to stay the night there. "There may be need for a flight first thing in the morning," I told her. "I don't think I could get back to Wapenamanda now, anyway."

The baby was born at about 8:00pm. Premature, but normal and healthy. There was great rejoicing.

But within minutes things had changed. The placenta had not come away, and the woman had begun to haemorrhage. Although there was no doctor present, the three experienced nursing sisters knew what to do. But to no avail. The retained placenta would not budge. And the bleeding would not stop.

By radio we made contact with the gynaecologist in the regional centre at Mount Hagen. His shouted instructions came through speakers set up in the bedroom. But nothing helped. Surgical intervention was out of the question. There were no facilities for typing and transfusing blood.

"If you could get her to the Wapenamanda hospital they could remove the placenta and transfuse her," the Mount Hagen doctor said during a conversation at about 9:30pm.

Everybody looked at me.

Another night flight? This one would not be to a coastal town like Wewak, but through ranges of high mountains to make a landing at Wapenamanda, six thousand five hundred feet above sea level, at the narrow end of a steep valley. In the dark. It was a very different challenge.

"I'll take the vehicle and go up to the airstrip," I said. "I'll look at the sky. I'll check the fuel, and I'll come back and tell you what I think we should do."

I sat in the darkness, alone, on the wing of the plane checking the fuel contents. There was no double reserve this time. In fact, I had used up some of my reserve fuel getting to Kandep and hadn't left Wewak expecting a medical emergency. If I was unable to get to Wapenamanda I would not have enough left to fly the extra seventy-five minutes on to Madang, the nearest coastal town.

"Please give me wisdom, Father," I prayed. In my imagination I could hear the cry of a healthy baby and the pleas of a frightened mother, begging. "Help me. Help me."

Opening my eyes after praying, I looked around the full three hundred and sixty degrees of the horizon. It was completely dark. But in every quadrant of the sky, in turn, sometimes concurrently and sometimes very close, there were flashes of lightning. Storms enveloped the entire area. Everywhere.

It was an unmistakable answer to my prayer. But it was painful. Very painful. With a heavy heart I drove back to the mission house and told them. It simply couldn't be done. It was not possible to fly through mountainous country, through the severe storms, in a fragile aircraft in the blackness of that night. To do so would result in three certain deaths and the destruction of a plane.

In the middle of the night the mother died. We sat in the house, exhausted and overwhelmed with grief.

The only sound was the crying of a little baby girl.

Next morning, as soon as the rain stopped and the clouds lifted enough to fly, I went in search of her husband. He had been on trek, visiting people many miles away to the southwest. From village to village I flew, low over the houses, until I located him travelling along a dusty track on his motorcycle.

He waved excitedly, wondering, of course, why I was flying around and around above him.

That morning we had prepared a small package with a note explaining what had happened. Having attracted his attention, I opened my window and dropped the package, with a streamer attached, into the slipstream. From above I saw him retrieve it and watched as he read it. I can see him still, just standing there, unmoving.

There was no wave as I turned and flew off back to Kandep.

A good decision. A tragic result.

Some weeks later I received in the mail a large parcel from the New Zealand headquarters of the mission of my friends at Kandep. It was a magnificent coffee-table book filled with wonderful photos of their picturesque homeland.

On the flyleaf, the mission leader had written,

"To our dear friend and fellow servant, Max Meyers. One who makes good decisions."

To ask for wisdom in making decisions is the right of every believer.

7

Skin-deep Fear

God is love. Whoever lives in love lives in God, and God in him . . . There is no fear in love. But perfect love drives out fear.

1 John 4:16, 18

These were not ordinary passengers, these four Samberigi men.

Brown-skinned and muscular, they were mountain men of Papua New Guinea's Southern Highlands. But on this day they exhibited none of the strength and confidence that would mark them as warriors who should be taken seriously. They carried no weapons.

They were sick and needed treatment. The small mission clinic at Samberigi was insufficient, and knowing that I was planning to fly across the mountains to the north coast, the station nurse asked me to drop these men off along the way. Mendi, about twenty minutes' flying to the north-west, had a regional hospital.

As I fastened their seat belts, I explained as best I could what they should expect on this short flight. But they appeared very uneasy. This was to be their first flight ever. Even for the initiated, flying in Papua New Guinea is often a daunting experience. To these tribesmen, who had grown up in the Stone Age, it may be nothing short of terrifying. I noticed the deteriorating weather and thought it could be a daunting experience for me!

Soon after take-off, light rain began to paint its peculiar patterns on the windscreen. Earlier, on the way up from Wasua, my home base on the Fly River, the weather had been reasonably good. At least at a higher altitude. But now the clouds grew ominous atop the mountain peaks. If I climbed above them, it would be difficult to find a way down again. Particularly in the relatively confined space of the Mendi valley.

I headed north-west, tracing the winding path of the mighty Erave River gorge. To the left and to the right majestic peaks filled the sky. On a clear day this steep gorge would present a vista of great beauty. Today, the light was a diffused grey, the river white and turbulent. Misty rain, whipped by mountain winds, produced a strange, matted effect upon the valley walls, and the higher ridges were shrouded in cloud. From the cockpit of my Cessna it almost seemed as if I was flying into the throat of a very inhospitable grey tunnel.

I noticed a narrow space between the cloud and the ridge to my right and made a quick turn into the next valley with the wheels of the aircraft almost touching the ridge-top. I flew east along that valley, planning to regain my track farther up. Thus, in a zigzag fashion, valley by valley, I made my way towards Mendi.

For a while I wondered whether I would find Mendi at all. I wished that I had not agreed to make this diversion. It would have been simple to fly to the south out of Samberigi for a few miles to climb above the clouds, then to negotiate a way through the mountains to Wewak, my final destination.

Totally absorbed as the minutes ticked by, I paid no attention to my passengers. Suddenly I heard a sound coming from the back seat. It was a low, drawn-out moan! I turned back.

There in the back seat, locked together in an embrace of abject fear, were my three mountain men. Their three black, curly heads were close together, their faces beaded with perspiration. Three pairs of arms were locked together. And staring back at me, three terror-filled pairs of eyes. They were speechless with fear. And my faltering words of encouragement did little to comfort them.

If this flight's tough for me, how must they be feeling? I thought.

I glanced across to check on my fourth passenger, sitting in the front seat. He, however, had a completely different demeanour. I was surprised. He was staring ahead, contemplative and detached. Even casual.

"Yu no gat pret?" I asked him. ("Aren't you afraid?")

He turned and looked squarely into my eyes. His response was slow and deliberate. I think he'd asked himself the same question.

"Skin bilong mi tasol i pret." ("Only my skin is afraid.")

What? Only his skin?

I talked on.

"So only your skin is afraid?" I asked. "What about the rest of you?"

Pointing out of the window, he answered in his pidgin English with one of the most expressive and profound statements I have ever heard.

"I see the mountains," he said. "They are so close." He gestured with a wave of his hand.

"I see the trees and the rocks as they rush by. I see the rain, and I hear it beating on the glass. I see the clouds all around us. All I see brings fear to me. I didn't know that this big bird of yours shook like this as it flew along. There is much to be afraid of here."

69

Then with a smile he continued, "But my fear is only as deep as my skin."

"What about the rest of you?" I asked again. "What about under your skin?"

"I am not afraid under my skin," he said. "You see, I know the One who made the mountains. I know the One who made the rocks and the trees. I know the One who made the clouds and the rain for today. He has told me that I don't need to be afraid. Why? Because He lives in me. Inside my skin. And He has promised never to leave me. Because of that, I am not afraid."

He smiled at me. I grinned back at him, incredulous. What a fantastic 'show and tell' of true, heaven-sent faith.

Fear was understandable in this situation. It was absolutely consuming his three friends in the back seat. But not him.

Fear was not granted entry beneath his skin. God was there.

We are told in the Bible that a great mystery, hidden for generations, has been made known to those who know God, who belong to Him. That mystery is 'Christ in you, the hope of glory.' My Samberigi friend also demonstrated another truth.

The 'Christ in you' is the victor over fear.

But it has to be believed. That is the faith part. Faith translates truth into reality. My Papua New Guinean passenger proved that to me on that flight to Mendi. His faith in this indwelling God worked! Fear does not have to infiltrate the person in whom the Spirit of Christ lives.

The lesson for me that day was all the more meaningful as it was delivered by this unique man, this extraordinary teacher. He had never sat in a classroom. He had never studied at a Bible college. But he knew God – and his faith was firm. The situation in which he found himself was far beyond any previous experience he had had. It was certainly beyond his control. It was as far removed from his cultural norm, his daily environment and his comfort zone as one could possibly imagine. It was terrifying for his friends. But his belief in God gave him the ability to cope.

"Skin tasol" – only skin needs to be afraid!

We who live in what could be described as the more sophisticated world also encounter circumstances beyond our control. We too find ourselves operating outside our comfort zone. Our fear may not be generated in a small aircraft negotiating the weather-filled high mountains of some faraway tropical country. Our testing place may be in the arena of a relationship that is damaged to a point where agony of heart seems perpetual. It may come because of painful tensions in marriage or in the agonising grief and loss of someone deeply loved. It may be the nagging worry over wayward children. It may be a medical diagnosis of a disease that has the power to threaten and even end life. It may be in the gut-wrenching tension of business. Or in the erosion of financial security. A host of things can bring great fear to our lives, fear that so easily will permeate the very fibre of our being, far deeper than our skin, and leave us wondering whether there is any hope of survival.

The God of heaven had become the personal God of my Samberigi passenger. And, now, his fear was only on the surface – skin-deep. Because not only was he able to understand great and profound truth, but he was also applying it to life. Rare? Sadly, all too rare. But available, nonetheless, to all. "Fear not. For I am with you," says the Lord. "For I have not given you a spirit of fear, but of love, and a sound mind."

I still like the way my friend put it.

"Skin bilong mi tasol i pret."

8

Hope on a River's Edge

And hope does not disappoint us, because God has poured out his love into our hearts by the Holy Spirit, whom he has given us.

Romans 5:5

"Can we really land down there?"

A muddy river snaked its way through heavily timbered slopes, which rose magnificently on both sides. I made a low run to measure the length of water available. The river ran fast. I could get down. Easily. The judgment call was whether I could get off again. Another timed, low-level run along the river gave me the confidence I needed. There were no rocks or swirling whirlpools, no tree trunks protruding from the river bank. The length of available water was okay.

This was flying at the ragged edge. There was no control tower, no support system, no one to help if anything went wrong. Only a narrow, murky river winding its way through a steamy jungle plateau in the mountains.

This was flying at its best. This was what I loved! Untidy as it is! The Air Force had offered nothing like this!

As the keel of the floats kissed the surface of the river with the familiar 'hiss', we had no way of knowing what we were about to confront.

The floats settled deeper into the water. Moments later, we sat mid-river, the little plane dwarfed by a huge, overhanging canopy of trees. Tresses of drooping vines formed giant curtains of green, screening an ancient and pristine forest.

The eastern reaches of the Erave River in Papua New Guinea seemed a century away from anywhere.

But just seventy miles away lay Kapuna, where the story begins.

Like many other Papua New Guinean villages, Kapuna wasn't a particularly pleasant place to live. Every day heat and humidity hovered together around the mid-thirties. The nights brought little respite. Remote and primitive, it was hardly a place for two brilliant doctors.

But Peter and Lyn Calvert were not ordinary people.

These 'Delta Doctors' had raised their children there, in Kapuna. Their house, constructed mainly of crude materials cut from the surrounding bush, looked much the same as all the other village houses. It stood perched on large log stilts high above the ground to keep it clear of the water that at high tide often inundated the entire village. Their furniture was of rough-hewn jungle wood. Fine nets draped over each bed, providing the only protection from malaria-carrying mosquitoes. But mosquito nets captured the heat and made the nights all the more oppressive.

The hospital, also built mainly with material from the surrounding jungle, was the essence of simplicity.

But the medical service the Calverts provided was of the highest order. It came with few of the trappings of the sophisticated hospitals in which they had trained and served. But there, in Kapuna, they conducted a nursing school, sharing their knowledge with scores of young women and men who came from villages hundreds of miles away to be educated in medical practices.

And from that unique little place the Calverts reached out.

The people of every isolated village, every hamlet along the hundreds of miles of rivers and steamy swamps became the object of their devotion. Their transportation was as basic as the environment in which they worked. No smart luxury vehicles. No trappings of success. In long wooden canoes hacked from jungle logs, they spent tedious hours, sitting at the stern, a hand wrapped around the throttle of an outboard motor. From village to village they travelled, delivering babies, dispensing medications, binding wounds, suturing gashes, diagnosing and treating all manner of disease and sickness.

Their children, in turn, also spent many hours in those canoes, schooled en route in correspondence lessons by Mum or Dad.

Though remote and isolated, Peter and Lyn were known by their voices all across the country. Each day they conducted a noon-hour medical clinic by high-frequency radio transceiver. Sometimes barely discernable above the scrambled static, diagnoses were made and treatment recommendations given. And on stations hundreds of miles away, mission nurses and medical workers strained to hear. No one could have been more respected and loved by so many. But they never met the Calverts, other than on the radio.

MAF longed to help them. We were able to offer our service and support to hundreds of other mission medical personnel around the country. But not to those at Kapuna. Not to the Calverts. There was no dry land there to make into an airstrip, even the few hundred yards required for our Cessnas. The whole region was one vast expanse of rivers and swamps.

But in 1967, our dream became a reality. We decided to remove the undercarriage from one of our Cessna 180 land planes and fit it with floats. This gave us access to many areas where airstrips were impossible to build. New people were reached, new areas opened.

Kapuna, in the hot and steamy Papuan Gulf, was accessible.

And so a new era of medical work began at Kapuna. Nursing teams came from surrounding regions. Graduates of the nursing school came back for concentrated periods. The float plane would fly teams from one village to another – an airborne shuttle-service of compassion and care.

Quickly, the value of our service became apparent. Utilising our aircraft, the Calverts could cover the major part of an entire year's village visitation schedule in eight days of concentrated work. Time formerly consumed by such slow, tedious travel could now be spent in more productive work.

It was just a year or so later that Peter Calvert, who was always on the lookout for some means to extend the limits of his extraordinary work, began talking about exploring new areas. He talked of people who lived far away to the north – in places never before reached by white men.

I had thought that the area he had in mind was uninhabited. It was a wild, forgotten area, densely timbered. A series of huge waterfalls and raging rapids made river contact from the swampy flatlands of the coastal belt impossible. There was a heavy population in the highland valleys away to the west and the north. But this was 'halfway' territory. It was 'no man's land'.

Peter insisted that we fly there to take a look. And he was not easily put off.

Having removed the back seats and all unnecessary weight from the aircraft to lighten it as much as possible, the two of us took off on this new adventure. Peter read the map excitedly, looking along the way for any evidence of humanity. Privately I was thinking to myself that the journey would be a waste of time.

To the west the river roared in a torrent. The plane couldn't land there. To the east there were many waterfalls and rapids.

I couldn't land there. But on this high plateau near some smaller mountains, I could land. And there were, indeed, people. Their small hamlets were clearly visible from the air.

Peter was right.

Having gingerly set the plane down on the water, we felt a sense of excitement.

The men of the village, all naked, peered at us. There were no women to be seen. No children. We assumed from past experience that they were hidden in the surrounding jungle, frightened by this huge, noisy bird.

These tough highland warriors waved their menacing spears, bows and arrows, and heavy clubs.

We taxied past the first group. They ran through the jungle to augment the group that waited around the bend at the second group of houses. As we continued by, they too ran off through the jungle to augment the next group. Rounding the last bend of this quiet section of the river, we saw a hundred or so men waiting.

We hoped it was a friendly greeting party.

I shut down the engine and steered the plane to the muddy shore. After securing it firmly we climbed the bank with uncertain smiles. This was scary. But the men appeared to be as apprehensive as we were.

With weapons in hand they surrounded us. One stepped forward slowly and tentatively. He touched our skin, then began feeling our bodies all over!

It was a meeting of two worlds. A young man stood leaning on a crudely fashioned crutch. Wrapped around his leg was a matted mess of grass and leaves. "He probably has nothing more than an untreated tropical ulcer," Peter explained to me. Then opening his medical bag and kneeling on the ground beside the man, he gently cut away the primitive bandage. The leg was swollen and inflamed. The wound was red, but tinged with grey, putrid, rotting flesh.

The man grimaced, then cried out in pain. Shouts of strong rebuke accompanied the slapping noise of arrows being placed at the ready.

"Leave him alone."

But Peter kept working slowly, carefully. He filled a shiny kidney-shaped dish with sterile water and tenderly washed that horrible sore. The man moaned, trying to be strong. I watched in silence. The tension was almost palpable.

But Peter's tenderness was obvious. The arrows, one by one, were put away. Soon these jungle warriors were squatting on their haunches around us, a sure demonstration that they no longer felt threatened.

Heads began to nod. There was whispered conversation. They had never seen compassion from a stranger.

Having cleansed the wound, Peter used an atomiser to puff sulphur powder into it. He gave the boy an injection of antibiotic. Gasps of amazement came from the men as he bound the leg with a pure white bandage.

The work was done. A bridge . . . of compassion . . . had been built. Friendship was established.

We showed them our plane and toured their village, catching sight of an occasional female face staring from the jungle.

Words weren't possible, but we explained to them that we would return in a month. We drew pictures in the sand with a stick. Thirty lines, one for each day in the lunar cycle. We scratched pictures of the phases of the moon between those lines, and then, pointing to the crescent moon in the blue sky, we told them that we would come back when the moon was once again in its present setting. They understood.

By the time we climbed aboard our little Cessna, we were like old and treasured friends. As we sped by on the take-off run, they were waving excitedly. We were soon on our way back to Kapuna.

What a day it had been.

And one month later, to the day, with the crescent moon against the blue sky, Peter and I returned.

To our astonishment, the village had been totally transformed. Women and children were there with the men at our landing place. Bodies glistened with fat and tree oil; heads and arms were adorned with feathers and crimson and yellow flowers. These new friends of ours yelled and waved their welcome. Women lined a path from the river bank to the centre of the village where the older men awaited us. We felt like VIPs inspecting a military guard of honour as we walked between the rows of excited, laughing women.

Every house in the village was decorated with the same crimson and yellow flowers. The assembled elders greeted us ceremoniously. They led us, with great pride, to a brand-new house they had built for us!

Into 'our' new home they brought the sick and the wounded. Men and women, the young and the old. And Peter cared for them there.

Our former patient needed no further treatment. His leg had healed. He stood watching, almost preening, without his crutch. His was a joyful pride.

At noon they had a feast prepared for us, a delicious meal of chicken cooked in coconut cream. It was worthy of inclusion on the menu of any five-star restaurant.

We saw no fear. There was none of the apprehension of the previous month. Instead we saw excitement. Most of all, we saw hope!

A month earlier, with primitive and awkward gestures, we had said that we would come back. But did they believe it? Would they just sit and talk about it? And hope? Or would they do something in preparation for our return?

They had decided to put their hope into action. It was apparent. They had planned for the day we would return.

They had worked hard throughout that month in preparation. They had decorated their village *with hope!*

Hope built that house for us. Hope did the cleaning. Hope gathered the flowers. Hope prepared the feast.

In their limited understanding they only saw that what we brought was physical healing. Their hope was that this would continue. And it did.

Yet the day was coming when they were to see the miracle of a deeper hope. The hope of spiritual healing. And, in time, they received that hope as well. Faith in God through Jesus.

'Our' home became the home of their first pastor. For a time it was also their church. And many of those people became evangelists, carriers of the hope they had found, to others in that remote area.

And that is another wonderful story.

9

Two Small Sticks

May I never boast except in the cross of our Lord Jesus Christ.

Galatians 6:14

Like so many other thousands of the people of Papua New Guinea, the people of Lake Kuvanmas had no outside contact. They lived in total isolation.

I had flown over Kuvanmas hundreds of times. A beautiful, deep, black-water lake nestling in the foothills on the northern side of the ranges, it had often been a welcome navigational fix after long periods of flying above the clouds.

Many times, on a routine flight into the mountains I had looked down at a village by the lake and wondered about its people. What were they like? What did they make of my noisy aircraft, a speck in the sky above? What were their beliefs and customs?

Our first contact with the people of Kuvanmas came mid-morning of a tranquil day, with the bright sun high in the sky overhead. Landing a float plane there offered no operational obstacles. The lake was long and broad.

The people there welcomed us with warmth. After showing us around their village they invited us into their homes. I almost had to get down on to my hands and knees to enter the doorway of the house to which I was taken.

It was round, about forty feet in diameter. The walls were made of split tree trunks about ten inches wide, tied together with jungle vine. Thatched grass formed the conical shaped roof, bare earth the floor.

Inside, the house was very dark, and initially I could see nothing but the red embers of cooking fires smouldering in the centre of the single room. Thin shafts of light from holes in the roof pierced the smoke-filled air, creating parallel streaks of grey-white in the darkness. Chinks of light also shone from spaces between the timbers of the walls. In time I could make out woven food bags, fishing nets and other equipment hanging from the roof. Bows and arrows leaned against the wall by the door. Blackened clay cooking pots and other household utensils were stacked close to the fire.

Slowly, as my eyes became accustomed to the darkness, I began to make out the grinning smiles of mummified human corpses, like a silent macabre audience, seated, with folded arms and crossed legs, around the walls of the house.

Emerging from the darkness, a boy, about twelve, came forward. He placed something in my hand. It was heavy. It felt like a stone, but I couldn't see it clearly. I shifted forward to catch a shaft of light on my hand. It was indeed a stone, a round, smooth piece of granite. But carved deeply into the surface of this stone, as if by some ancient hand, was the figure of a strange, semi-human face.

I had seen such things before, but only rarely. To these people, carved stones like this were sacred things. They represented the spirits of their ancestors and were never shown to outsiders.

"What's the significance of this stone," I asked, "and why are you showing it to me?"

"It's a spirit stone," he replied, stumbling with the unfamiliar pidgin language we were using. "This stone is the spirit of my *tumbunas* . . . my ancestors."

I asked him how it was that he, a young boy, came to possess such a thing, let alone show it to me. They were usually only in the care of family elders or those who had a special spiritual role among the people. They were never the playthings of children. He explained to me that his father and uncles were all dead and so the guardianship of this sacred stone had been passed down to him.

"But now . . . I no fear. I know other spirit God. He is true. He . . . strong!" he added confidently in his broken pidgin English.

Then he retreated into the darkness. I wondered what he would bring back to me this time. Returning, he placed something else in my hand. Sticks? Moving again to the same shaft of light, I was astonished to see what he had brought to me.

Two small sticks were crudely tied together to form a cross.

"This isn't from the time of your *tumbunas*," I exclaimed to him. "It's just two sticks tied together."

Now, more animated, he proceeded to tell me in an excited way about the life of Jesus! He told me of healing and other miracles. He told me that the wooden cross had to do with Jesus' death, that it was on something like this that he died.

Trying to ascertain the extent of his understanding, I asked him why anyone, let alone a god, would allow men to kill him when he had the power to escape death. He explained that this was not an ordinary man. He was God. He was not a spirit who lives in a carved stone. He can't be defeated or overcome by the power of another family's spirit. And He had to die. He died for the people who killed Him. Then he added, "He died for me."

I could hardly believe what I was hearing. God was already there at Kuvanmas in the life of this young boy!

As I asked him more about the life and death of Jesus, he was able to answer, simply but confidently. His belief and faith in God were remarkable.

This was a primitive, untouched place. These were people of an ancient culture. To this boy, my world of relative sophistication was entirely unknown. Yet we shared an astounding commonality across a broad cultural gap. We were poles apart in background, in age and experience. But in that unforgettable meeting, God brought together two of His children who shared a great treasure.

I told him that I too knew the same story of Jesus, that He was my God as well.

"What missionary told you about Jesus?" I inquired. But he didn't even know the word *missionary*! Or the word *pastor*, or *evangelist*. He certainly didn't have a Bible. There had been no presentation of the Good News at Kuvanmas. I was amazed. "How did you hear?" I asked him. "Who told you?" His response, his story, was amazing.

He told me something of the culture of his people and explained their system of trade. Certain periods of the year were allocated for barter between the tribal groups. Territorial barriers, normally crossed only at the threat of death, were opened and free travel was allowed.

The Kuvanmas people, for instance, had an abundance of meat. They hunted in the surrounding forests and dried and cured meat in village smokehouses. But they had no clay to make cooking pots. They lacked other essentials as well. So as the time of open trade approached, they stockpiled their smoke-dried meat and then took it many miles through the forest and across vast wetland areas to the Sepik River. There the people had plenty of fish but very little red meat. They also had plenty of clay in their homeland, so the Sepik people exchanged with the people of Kuvanmas clay cooking pots for dried red meat.

My new friend told me of his travelling with the trading party, day after day, through the swamps and down the rivers until they reached the faraway Sepik River village where the exchange of goods traditionally took place. What an adventure for a young man!

The bartering sessions were carried out with great seriousness and complex ritual. Young boys were not allowed to attend; consequently he was forced to wait outside in that strange, unfamiliar, even hostile village.

"The ceremonies went on for three days," he explained. "I made friends with a Sepik boy about my own age. We talked much. We sat by the river and in his house. And we walked through his village, talking together. He told me the story of Jesus. He told me about this one who is truly God. We talked of almost nothing else. It was there I believed. It was there we made this cross."

The grinning, mummified faces and the parallel shafts of light in the dark, smoky air added impact to the telling. What a marvellous story of God's love, reaching into the most unexpected places. Just as the sun shone a ray of light through the roof above me, so God's love had shone into the heart of one young boy through the life and faith of another.

Just two sticks!

10

Triumph and Tragedy at Tifalmin

*The light shines in the darkness, but the darkness has not
understood it . . . The true light that gives light to every
man was coming into the world . . . Yet to all who received
him, to those who believed in his name, he gave the right
to become children of God – children born not of natural
descent, nor of human decision or a husband's will, but
born of God.*

John 1:5, 9, 12–13

Tifalmin was breathtakingly beautiful.

The rugged peaks to the west reaching up to fourteen
thousand feet were often lost in billowing clouds. The
mountains to the north and to the south, though no less
rugged, lowered progressively to seven thousand feet to the
eastern end of the valley. The river, which curled its way
eastwards through the valley, was the run-off of almost daily
storms that drenched the mountains. The river finally threw
itself over a waterfall, filling the air with a misty spray.

From above, the valley seemed a place of peace. Smoke of
a hundred cooking fires rose lazily above the trees, softening
the tranquil scene with a blue-grey haze.

The airstrip at Tifalmin had been cut from timbered land
alongside the river in the centre of the valley. For the many

hands, thousands of hands, it had not been light work. Barely five hundred yards long, with rising ground at the western end, the airstrip left no room for error. One learnt to place the aircraft's wheels on the stony ground right at the airstrip's threshold. It was a one-way airstrip. There was no 'go-around', no second chance.

The Cessna seemed so delicate and fragile against the towering mountains. It was a hostile environment for flying. The upward thrust of warm tropical air forced aloft by the rugged terrain could bring rapid change to weather conditions. Flying here called for more than the normal vigilance.

Tifalmin was no place for a Saturday afternoon recreational pilot.

But Tifalmin is most memorable for me not because of its unique beauty or because of the challenge of landing an aircraft there. Tifalmin is memorable because of its people, memorable because in that valley I would witness the triumph of God. But, as well, people I knew and loved would pay the greatest of all human sacrifice.

The piercing, challenging, unflinching stares from the men were my first impression of these people. Their eyes, with a peculiar redness, perhaps the result of living in smoke-filled houses, issued a clear warning. This environment belonged to them. It was their valley, their world. They were the masters. Little covered their nakedness. Long gourds, secured with a thin woven cord around the waist like athletic straps, rather than cover their nakedness seemed only to accentuate it!

Most of them wore two black feather quills inserted into holes punctured in the side of each nostril. These quills crossed in the centre of their foreheads. Many had whitened bones or a large pig's tooth inserted horizontally through the stretched septum of the nose. The biceps of some of the men were wound with what seemed like blackened and withered sinews, the sex organs of wild boars. They were the mark of the great hunter and were worn with pride.

There was no shame, no coyness about these men. Only pride.

The weapons they carried also created an immediate impression. Black palm bows were strung with cane bowstring capable of taking as much tension as those strong, muscled arms could produce. Arrows designed for a variety of targets were carried, always at the ready. Some arrows, tipped with hard, black palm wood and finely sharpened bone, were intricately carved and painted with rich brown ochre.

These were for the killing of men.

The women were different. Their clothing was skimpy, just a thick grass skirt no more than six inches in length hanging in front, below the waist. Some wore a similar skirt at the back. Even so, this brief covering seemed more modest than that of the men. And the ladies of Tifalmin were coy, shy, lowering their heads and turning away upon eye contact with strangers.

The women were the workers, the gardeners of the community. They bore the evidence of this special role. Their hands were cracked and gnarled, their bodies well-encrusted with the rich volcanic earth of that remarkably fertile place.

Children were everywhere. Dirty babies suckled dirty breasts. A baby not suckling was carried in a woven string bag suspended from the forehead and hanging down the back of its mother. Other bags, similarly slung over the head, contained food and other household necessities. Older children, carried on the hips of their mothers, gnawed on pieces of sweet potato.

The women of Tifalmin were tough. They did the hard physical work.

The houses were well constructed of material from the surrounding bush. Round, with only one room, they were double walled of woven, beaten bamboo. The densely thatched grass roof entrapped smoke from the permanent fire inside and allowed it to escape only in lazy, fine wisps which to the unfamiliar gave, from the outside, the impression that the house was slowly smouldering away.

It was the women who took most of our attention on the first day I visited Tifalmin. It was 'mothers-and-babies' day. And two of my passengers were nurses who came here regularly to conduct an infant-welfare clinic. My other passenger was a male missionary, faced with the long-range challenge of creating relationships with the men.

There was a lot of chatter as the day got underway. The old-fashioned, round-faced scale that was hung over a low branch of a nearby tree seemed more designed for weighing garden produce than babies. A portable table was erected upon which the tools of the nurses' trade were laid out . . . stethoscope, auriscope, forceps, syringes, scissors, and so forth.

Despite much protesting and noisy howling, each baby was weighed. The auriscope was used to check the babies' ears. There was a careful feeling of the spleen for any swelling or tenderness in that area, a certain indication of malaria. Each mother was questioned closely about feeding and other important indicators of good mother-baby care. Some babies were given injections, always to the familiar cries of protest.

Ear infections were rampant among children at Tifalmin. With each family living in a one-roomed house, a baby's crying was often the cause of domestic tension, so the Tifalmin women would take a small beetle, which, when placed in the ear of a crying baby, could be guided to crawl down into the aural canal. Its movement would bring soothing relief, albeit temporarily, to the baby. I have watched on a number of occasions as those nurses, with great care, removed a rotten grey mess of dead beetles from a little baby's ear.

Infant mortality brought its own special anguish to the mothers of Tifalmin.

Our activity on one end of the parking bay was 'women's stuff'. The men, armed and dangerous-looking, sat around small fires on the other end. There was little talk. They were not relaxed. Their bows and wicked-looking arrows were held close, always at the ready. Treachery was the mark of stature among the men. Fear kept their horizons small and defences strong. Life was cheap, often snatched away by sickness and infection about which they knew so little. Or by enemy tribes.

They listened attentively, nevertheless, to the missionary's stories about creation, about heaven and earth, about God. They themselves were also great storytelling people. But while the women were literally pouring out their love and gratitude for the care they were receiving, the men, still with their weapons close at hand, remained serious, unsmiling. We had invaded their territory.

At the end of the day they stood still and gazed intently as my passengers squeezed back into the plane for the return to Telefomin. It was a short flight, only five minutes, and hardly worth an entry in a logbook. But it had nevertheless been a flight spanning a thousand years, a flight into the Stone Age.

When I flew back to Wewak, I said to Jo, "The medical work is amazing. And so deeply appreciated. But the teaching, the mission work – that's a different matter. It will take generations before a result is seen."

We were in the business of bringing the light to Tifalmin, but as Scripture says, "The darkness did not understand it."

Two years later, on a Sunday morning, I stood again by that same beautiful river at Tifalmin. Many hundreds of the villagers had gathered there. They looked the same, wore exactly the same scant clothing. But by this time something was different.

There were no scrutinising and distrusting stares. No challenging, piercing eyes demanding that we look away. And as a greater contrast – there were no bows, no arrows, no clubs. There were no weapons at all.

I waded into the crystal-clear, cold water to sit on a rock a few yards from the shore, and somewhere, someone began to sing. It was nothing familiar, and not in a melodic form familiar to my Western ear. A strange tribal chant. But it was a rich and beautiful song that gladdened the heart of God. Then, as the singing continued, one by one, thirty or so of those Tifalmin people, women and men, waded out into that river pool to be baptised.

The valley looked the same. The same grey-blue smoke rose lazily to paint the valley with early morning haze. The mountains still rose from the east with their black western peaks disappearing into billowing masses of cloud. The same sparkling river wended its way through the valley to throw itself in a mass of spray over that last rock face.

But Tifalmin was not the same. The corner of a heavy blanket of fear and darkness had been lifted. The light had come. It had penetrated that beautiful little valley and had begun to make things new!

Later that afternoon I sat in my aircraft, the engine already started, running down the pre-take-off checklist. Through the whirling blades of the propeller I could see a group of Tifalmin people. I could see the loving smiles of the women and the laughing grins of those mountain warriors – my friends.

It seemed as if I could hear a clear, resonating voice from above the clouds that were beginning to fill the valley, an almost audible benediction.

"You are a chosen people, a royal priesthood, a holy nation, a people belonging to God, that you may declare the praises of him who called you out of darkness into his marvellous light."

Walt and Vonnie Steinkraus, translators with Wycliffe Bible Translators, died at Tifalmin village in 1971. With their three children!

The Steinkrauses had come from America to live at Tifalmin as the church came to life. From the air their house was hardly discernible from all the other village houses. Its only distinguishable feature was two lengths of corrugated iron sheeting laid on the roof to catch rainwater and channel it into two fifty-gallon drums that stood outside the house.

Walt and Vonnie went without modern conveniences. They lived simply, identifying as much as possible with the lifestyle of the people. Skilled in linguistics, they were committed to the long and arduous task of reducing the hitherto unrecorded language to print and then to the even more challenging task of translating into that language the Word of God.

Vonnie Steinkraus grew roses at Tifalmin. The fertile soil of that highland valley responded well to her green fingers, and on a number of occasions I flew away across the mountains towards home carefully sheltering a single cut rose under the pilot's seat. A rose was a treasure for Jo in humid, tropical Wewak.

Tifalmin was a lonely place for the Steinkraus family. It was far from the ordinary. But Walt and Vonnie Steinkraus were not ordinary people. The Steinkrauses had long-range plans.

Sunday was always a non-flying day for MAF, but we made ourselves available for emergency flights. Early on a Sunday morning one of the staff would receive and deal with any requests received on the HF radio. Usually these would be medical emergencies only.

On this particular Sunday a radio message came from Telefomin. It was a strange message: "There are calls of anguish and distress being shouted from village to village saying that something very serious has happened at Tifalmin. Could you please come to fly us over there?"

Within minutes I was on my way, climbing towards the dark, rugged peaks ahead. Upon arrival at Telefomin, the turnaround was rapid, and I was soon headed towards Tifalmin with friends from the Baptist Mission as my passengers.

The valley presented its usual tranquil, smoky calm. It wasn't until we flew over the airstrip that we saw it.

It was stark evidence of a horrible disaster. Across the valley, on the other side of the river opposite the village, thousands of tons of sodden earth and rock had fallen away from high ground there. It had somehow been projected outwards with such enormous force that it had literally rained down from above, on to the village of Tifalmin.

Tifalmin village no longer existed.

In its place were acres of brown, oozing mud about twenty feet thick. Thousands of protruding tree trunks, like snapped limbs, punctured the surface, along with branches, bushes and rocks. The only houses that had escaped destruction were a few which had been at the periphery of the village. The rest of the village, the church, the school, the Steinkraus house – all were gone, obliterated, crushed and buried under thousands of tons of mud.

In what remained of the parking bay, a group of Tifalmin people jumped and waved, imploring us to come down to their help.

There was barely enough airstrip for a very short precautionary landing. Half of the airstrip was similarly engulfed in this sodden mess.

I stopped with the aircraft's spinning propeller only feet from a twenty-foot wall of mud.

We were surrounded by a wailing, grieving, sorrowing group of our Tifalmin friends, weeping for their lost village, for their family members whose lives had been taken and who were still buried in that horrible, sodden mass.

Distraught, they wept also for Walt and Vonnie and all three of the Steinkraus children. "They're under there, lost and crushed," they cried.

We slithered and climbed our way to the top of that brown wet hill. For hundreds of yards we could see nothing but thick mud.

"After our time of worship in the church," the people said, "most of us went to secure and cut a large log that was caught in a downstream bend of the river. A few of the older people went back to their houses and did not come. The Steinkrauses went to their house too. Now, all who stayed in the village are lost."

We dug through that mud hour after hour, every day for three days. But our searching was in vain. The thick mass of mud was quickly hardening, impacting in the daytime heat.

It was heart-wrenchingly sad when on the second day we located the body of a beautiful little girl, the youngest of the Steinkraus children. Hers was the only body to be recovered there.

Early on the Sunday morning she had been lovingly dressed for church, all in white. Somehow in death she had been protected from the engulfing mud and rocks by one of the sheets of galvanised iron on the roof. Her little body was barely scratched, hardly dirty in the midst of such filth.

We were a quiet and sombre group as we laid her gently back into the mud. It seemed best that she remain there with the rest of her family.

No trace of anyone else was found.

There was only one eyewitness to the disaster, an elderly lady. I was standing by her as she was questioned through an interpreter by a senior government official, one of many people I had shuttled to Tifalmin in the three days following the disaster.

"What did you see?" he asked her.

"I saw the earth falling from the sky upon our home," she replied. "So I ran away down the airstrip, but then I stopped to pray."

"Pray?" came the question. "What on earth did you pray for?"

"I prayed," she said, "that God would take only those who already knew Him. I asked Him not to allow anyone to die who didn't yet know Him. I asked Him to take only those who would go to heaven."

This simple mountain woman understood life. She understood death. She understood eternity.

Some years later when I was recounting these events to an Australian friend, he shared with me a wonderful postscript to the Steinkraus story.

As a student my friend John had flown to Papua New Guinea to help in the building of an airstrip in another valley and was working under the direction of Walt Steinkraus. They became close friends. At the completion of their time together, as John was leaving for home, Walt gave him a signed family photo. The Scripture reference Walt Steinkraus pencilled on the photograph was Psalm 40:2. It says:

He lifted me out of the slimy pit, out of the mud and the mire; he set my feet on a rock and gave me a firm place to stand.

Could Walt Steinkraus have had a premonition about his family's death? I don't think so. But from their tomb of mud in the beautiful valley of Tifalmin that Sunday morning, Walt, Vonnie and their children were lifted, by the Psalmist's

God, out of the mud and the mire. Their feet were set upon a rock, and He gave to them a firm place to stand, clean before Him.

I saw tragedy at Tifalmin . . . tragedy in human terms. But I saw triumph at Tifalmin . . . triumph in eternal terms.

It is such a little place. It is so insignificant, almost unnoticeable.

But not to God.

11

No-nonsense Faithfulness

Then Jesus came to them and said, "All authority in heaven and on earth has been given to me. Therefore go and make disciples of all nations, baptising them in the name of the Father and of the Son and of the Holy Spirit, and teaching them to obey everything I have commanded you. And surely I am with you always, to the very end of the age."

Matthew 28:18–20

Dick Donaldson was a unique individual.

He invariably looked the same. Same shorts, same short-sleeved shirt, same work boots and socks and, always, a felt hat. I suppose it was appropriate. But it was always the same.

Dick didn't smile a lot. Except with his eyes, that is.

In those pioneer days of mission work, when the plane provided the only link to the outside world, warm words of thanks and gestures of appreciation were frequent rewards of the pilot.

But not from Dick. "Thanks," he would say. "See you next trip," and he would load a wheelbarrow with supplies we had unloaded from the aircraft and wheel it off along the narrow track to the mission house a few hundred yards away.

A taciturn man, Dick would, however, from time to time, involve me in discussion about theological matters. He loaned me a book one day, saying, "Read this, Meyers. It'll do you good. You might not agree with it, but you'll be wrong."

Living where he did, doing what he did, Dick was not internationally known. I could write about any one of the thousands of missionary men and women I have served who have been wonderfully used by God. Dick Donaldson was no 'cover story' missionary with a beaming smile.

On the contrary, he was argumentative, aggressive and tough. He had an air of authority and was confident in what he was doing. He lived out obedience and faithfulness and was prepared to pay the heavy cost of his calling. Without question.

Dick was committed to the Orokana people – and they knew it. The church at Orokana emerged from that primitive society, strong and secure. It had the brush of Donaldson solidarity about it, the same qualities of spiritual life and strength.

We are told that faith can move mountains. Dick Donaldson had moved a mountain. Well, almost! He had built the airstrip at Orokana by moving countless tons of earth. Cutting here, filling there. Every available foot of space on a gently sloping hillside was utilised. Operationally, it was not the easiest of airstrips. It left no margin for pilot error. But it was adequate. And the airstrip was Orokana's lifeline. The Orokana people were the Donaldsons' people. More importantly, the people claimed the Donaldsons as their very own.

Every time I climbed away from Orokana, even after a ten-minute stop, I always had a sense of privilege in being able to serve Dick Donaldson. To me, he was a 'father in the faith', a teacher, a role model, even a prophetic voice.

He didn't use many words. But I knew he was appreciative,

and his occasional thin smile and wry sense of humour hid a man of joy and rich humour. And in his own unique way, he often gave me the urge to go on to develop and grow.

To Dick the task was urgent and serious. And he always had his sights on even more distant horizons.

The powerful Continental engine droned smoothly on. I made another turn and then another, following a patterned sequence over the vast, unending miles of jungle green. Dick and I were surveying a new area, hitherto untouched. We were sixty miles from Orokana.

With a sheet of paper spread between us, we were talking together, comparing various features visible from either side of the plane, making our map. We recorded every detail, every feature, traced the flow of every river, compared the position of every ridge. And every village.

Off to the south, dominating the landscape was a huge dormant volcano, Bosavi, rising majestically to over nine thousand feet above the plateau. Although its apex for weeks at a time was lost in thick clouds, Bosavi made a superb reference point.

"Go down to about a thousand feet," Dick said, after a time.

We had drawn our map thus far with the broad strokes of features visible from a higher altitude. Now we had to draw in the finer details. From the lower altitude we could clearly see that each of the 'villages' we had observed comprised a few smaller structures surrounding one huge communal dwelling. Each house was built on heavily timbered slopes. Huge vertical logs provided secure protection at the Gout with the family area, an 'open porch' at the rear, high above the steeply sloping ground.

By sheer size, each house must have contained many families.

Yet as we flew by, lower again this time, there was not a living soul visible. From one village to another. We knew they were there. Women and children would be well hidden and protected in the surrounding jungle, and the men watching through the trees. The aircraft, an unknown creature from far away, with its strange noise, seemed to be searching for them.

It was.

And they hid.

The map had been drawn, the population judgments made; our work was complete. Now the difficult work began. We must find a site for an airstrip.

From the air we had observed that while all around, the timber was heavy and dense, there were cleared areas on the faces of a number of ridges. 'Slash and burn' garden sites were under cultivation, and others from previous years were still visible, though swiftly being reclaimed by the voracious forest. It was difficult to see how we could ever land this small Cessna anywhere in that jungle.

Eventually, we chose a site. It lay in a section of heavily timbered ground, sloping gently upwards along the foothills of Mount Bosavi.

"Now go down low," he said. "Fly over the four largest settlements, very low, very slow." He smiled and had a twinkle in his eye.

"Bring it down," he said. "Ten or twenty feet will do. But make it real slow. I want to have a close look."

I protested, but Dick was undeterred. "Come on, just do it."

So down we went.

Then, as we passed over the first of a number of selected 'long houses', Dick, to my astonishment, quickly opened the plane's window, took something from the rucksack he had on the floor between his legs, and dropped it out of the window.

"What on earth are you doing?" I cried. It was hardly an approved action. "What did you throw out of the window?"

With that characteristic thin smile, he opened the rucksack and showed me four or five very small cans. It was household paint. To each can he had attached a ribbon.

"It's all right for you," he said. "You can fly from Orokana to Bosavi in twenty-five minutes. It will take me weeks to get out here on foot! And it will be hard enough to see the sun, let alone navigate based upon this crude map we've just drawn. When I get here, how do you think I am going to match map with reality? There has to be a start-off point. I won't even be able to see Bosavi when I'm down there. But I'll tell you what! Those men down there are gonna pick up those cans. They probably already have the first one. I'd be surprised if they aren't already covered in paint. They love the stuff. They'll be the 'red people'."

So we proceeded, legally or not, merrily dropping cans of paint on to a string of villages. We marked the 'red village', the 'yellow village', and the 'green village', and so on, until his little sack of goodies was completely empty.

That day, a new light began to dawn over the rugged forest area of the Bosavi slopes. And as primitive men felt the oily texture of this strange paint and marked their arms and foreheads . . . and their houses . . . with its rich colour, they were unknowingly marked as those who would hear about the greatest outpouring of love that history has ever known.

The noise of the aircraft engine, a terrifying thunder to them on that first day, was to become, like an extended drum roll, the prelude to a beautiful symphony of love that would woo them out of darkness into a marvellous light.

The departure of the first Bosavi expedition was something to remember. It had taken many Cessna flights to gather all the people and supplies for this epic trek. There was Dick, same shorts, same short-sleeved shirt, same work boots and socks, same felt hat. Another mission colleague and about thirty or so men from the Orokana area joined him. They carried an incredible quantity of supplies. Metal lockers had been carefully packed. Through each of the long handles of these lockers, wooden poles had been inserted so they could be carried at shoulder height by two men walking the trail in tandem.

As the last of the men disappeared into the heavy jungle with days of arduous mountain travel ahead, I marvelled at their courage.

The forest site on the northern slopes of Bosavi slowly, very slowly, took on the appearance of an airstrip. From the air, I could see the criss-crossed trunks of felled trees and a small clearing where Dick's rough camp was established. Within a few weeks it was a gash in the forest, brown among the green. I had said to him, "Prepare a clearing a couple of hundred feet long. Then I'll be able to drop you what you need."

And so the 'darkness-to-light' project proceeded. Far away from home and family, alone among new-found but primitive friends, Dick worked. He addressed the gargantuan task with vigour. The airstrip was crucial to his plan.

With the plane's right-hand door removed, it was very noisy. Bags of supplies were balanced precariously on the door sill as I made the approach low over the tall trees at the upper end of the airstrip site. A quick descent brought us down farther, to just a few feet above the ground. The dispatcher, another mission friend, knelt on the floor of the plane. I yelled, "Now!" whereupon he pushed out as many bags as possible through the door before the signal to stop. The drop zone was short that first time. But it lengthened, week by week. Shovels, wheelbarrow components, crowbars, and of course food and mail for Dick . . . out they went!

He always recovered the mailbag first.

Dick's wife, Audrey, and his four wonderful kids, paid a high price for the Bosavi airstrip. But they paid it willingly. For they knew it was more than simply an airstrip. This was a down payment on the hearts of thousands of those Bosavi people.

What a great day of celebration it was when I made the very first landing on the Bosavi airstrip. The joy and amazement on the faces . . . the yelling . . . I shall never forget it.

They jostled with each other to get near my machine. They compared impressions as they stroked its cold, smooth surface. As I gazed out upon that sea of laughing, smiling brown faces, I saw him. I saw a felt hat.

I saw weariness on his face.

Soon, a young Australian family made Bosavi their home and began a programme of health, education, language acquisition and literacy. And they began to teach of the Word of God.

The Los Angeles Hilton is a long way from the rainforest of Bosavi. Most guests there would feel very uncomfortable if left at the Bosavi airstrip. To some, it would be like landing on another planet! But how would a Bosavi villager feel in the glitz and polish of the Hilton?

It was in 1991 that Jo and I drove from our Redlands home to Los Angeles to meet an Australian friend staying at the Hilton. We were delighted to find that he was travelling with a delegation of leaders from Papua New Guinea. There was much laughter and lively conversation as we shared with these men the happy memories of our many years in their beautiful country. They were very sophisticated, fluent in English, perfectly at ease in this renowned international hotel.

But in the background, one of the delegation stood quietly. He was shy and waited until some of the others moved away before stepping forward to speak to us.

Changing from English into the pidgin of his homeland, he asked Jo and me about our life in Papua New Guinea. His dark eyes were searching our faces as he asked about our work. Then, all of a sudden, when I mentioned my role in flying, his face instantly lit up with joy and recognition.

"Now I know who you are," he said. "I recognise your face. From Bosavi. I was there when you dropped that cargo from your plane. I worked for months on that airstrip! I cleared away bushes and trees! For weeks – for months – we waited for the day when the plane could land among us. All those weeks as you flew by we longed to meet you, to touch you, to touch your plane. You brought food for Mr Donaldson. You brought medicines for us. You brought us the help we needed so desperately. When the airstrip was made, you brought the Briggs family to live among us. That changed our lives."

And so he told us the Donaldson story from his perspective. It was not a story of a foreign religion being foisted upon a reluctant people. It was a story of a transformed people, a people no longer enshrouded in darkness, no longer behind the barriers of awful isolation and the stigma of cannibalism. It was a wonderful story of liberation, of an accelerated transition from the Stone Age to the twentieth century.

More importantly, he explained, it was the story of the Bosavi people of Papua New Guinea coming to realise that God was real, that He was the answer to their deepest need.

Our Bosavi friend told of his early education in a rough bush school at Bosavi. He talked of the influence of those missionaries and how they had brought an end to the fear that had bound the people for so long. He told us of how he had listened to the missionaries' stories – white man's stories – at first. He spoke of how it was that in time those same stories were really relevant and meaningful to him and demanded a personal response. He told us of the day he committed his life to Jesus.

He placed one hand over his heart and his other over mine, and then, clasping his hands together he said, "We come from different places, but we belong to each other."

As we parted, this dignified Papua New Guinean leader shook our hands with a beaming smile. In the opulence of the atrium of the Los Angeles Hilton we celebrated the wonder of the relationship we shared – in Christ.

I doubt if Dick Donaldson has ever been in the Los Angeles Hilton.

But it seemed to me that, somehow, he was represented there that night.

I could almost see his smile . . . under a felt hat!

12

Miracles and Monsters

Now to him who is able to do immeasurably more than all we ask or imagine, according to his power that is at work within us, to him be glory in the church and in Christ Jesus throughout all generations, for ever and ever! Amen.

Ephesians 3:20–21

Before the aircraft taxied to a stop, the smell was obvious. And for the mob of young Papua New Guinean kids who always chased our planes as we taxied in, it was a new and pungent odour.

"This is going to be interesting," I chuckled to myself as I undid my shoulder harness and stepped down to the ground.

Crowding around the plane, the children were soon joined by excited highland men and women, pushing and shoving, craning their necks to catch a glimpse of the amazing thing I had dragged from inside the cabin and now held suspended from my hand. Their yells and shouts of excitement drew more onlookers from the nearby government patrol post. Soon the little yellow plane was engulfed in a mass of brown, jostling, shouting people, wide-eyed with amazement. Their excited questions tumbled out one upon the other.

"Wanem dispela samting? Wanem kain abus? Mipela no lukim dispela bipo. Em i save kaikai man?" ("What is this? What kind

of creature? We've never seen anything like this before. Is it dangerous? Does it bite?")

It was only a fish.

But what a fish! Three feet of plump, sleek, silver barramundi. And it sure felt heavy, as with one hand I held it up by the gills for all to see. I had estimated its weight at probably thirty pounds. There was no scale to check it, and I had hoped that my calculations were correct as I loaded more than twenty similar fish into my Cessna 180 for the hour's flight from Lake Murray to the highlands.

To make the most of the impact, I unloaded the largest fish first. And as I took the others one by one from the plane, the gasps of astonishment increased. The pile of inert torpedo-shaped bodies, glistening in the sun, grew bigger. I pretended to throw one to a man at the front of the crowd. He fell back on the others behind him with a yell of fear. And they all came tumbling after! Much was the laughter at his embarrassment. Looking at something so totally foreign was one thing. Touching it was another thing altogether.

These were slippery, shiny creatures – with huge, glassy, staring open eyes. No legs, no feet, no arms, no hands, no fur or feathers or hair. Interesting, even intriguing. But the unknown brings caution; the unfamiliar, fear. So the people were wary about getting too close. They wanted to see, but only the brave would risk touching these strange, exotic, weird-smelling things.

Pigs, they knew. Pigs were treasured among the tribespeople of this land. They meant wealth! Birds they knew as well. Some birds were hunted for food, others for their rich and brilliantly coloured feathers. Special three-pronged arrows were made for the killing of birds. Cassowaries they knew. Cassowaries were a prized, but somewhat rare, source of food.

"Wanem dispela samting?"

I tried to explain to them that these things called 'fish' lived in water. Not in the fast-running, white-water mountain streams familiar to them, but in large lakes and in deep, slow-moving rivers. Any creatures living in their cold, swift creeks and rivers were very small – nothing like these huge fish. I also told them that they made excellent food.

The concept of the vastness of the ocean was beyond my ability to describe and theirs to understand. So I didn't even try.

The mission and government staff, of course, knew what I had brought. They were even more excited. Not in their wildest dreams had they ever expected to see huge fresh fish like these in their remote mountain station.

Thus, being a 'fish merchant' was added to the already long list of roles I filled in my work as an MAF pilot.

Keith Dennis was a New Zealander who had lived in Papua New Guinea since 1940 and had helped establish the work of his mission – then the Unevangelized Fields Mission (UFM), now Pioneers – at two different places along the mighty Fly River. He was one of those incredibly practical people who could turn his hand to anything. With the threat of the advancing Japanese army during World War II, he and the other missionaries in Papua New Guinea were forced to evacuate to safety. Keith had made the long river journey to the mission headquarters at Wasua and then on to New Zealand via Thursday Island at the tip of Cape York Peninsular, the northernmost point of Australia.

Returning at the end of the war he married his sweetheart, Lillian, and in 1948 they chose to serve among the people of the remote Lake Murray area, close to the border of what was to be later called Irian Jaya. They built a large, comfortable home and mission station from local bush material at Pangoa, a picturesque headland on the eastern shore of the lake.

'Dennis's Place' was to become a unique haven of hospitality.

Keith and Lillian had little or no contact with any Westerners in those early days. They saw their colleagues only at the annual conference of UFM. For many years the mission boat, the *M.V. Maino*, provided their only link to the outside world. It plied the long Fly River from Wasua, a tiny place near the river's mouth. To reach Pangoa, the *Maino* had to leave the Fly and sail for many miles up the Strickland, then the Herbert River and into Lake Murray.

The boat brought a variety of cargo for the Dennises. Building, medical and educational supplies sustained their work. Packaged or canned food supplemented what they grew or traded with the local people. Yet Lillian always welcomed guests, even though on occasions the menu might consist of sago, taro and crocodile meat! The Dennises knew how to live simply; they learned from the people at Lake Murray and adopted many of their ways.

But strangely, while their home was by a truly splendid tropical lake more than thirty miles in length, they had no fish.

No fish, in a lake like this?

Keith Dennis had been a keen fisherman in New Zealand and had eagerly anticipated the excitement and fun of fishing in Lake Murray. Fresh fish would wonderfully augment their somewhat restricted diet.

He often saw tiny fingerlings and schools of small, pointed-nose garfish in the shallow waters. *Where there are small ones, there must be large ones*, he thought. But apart from the occasional almost-inedible catfish, he caught nothing.

He fished the lake from one end to the other. He tried numerous types of gear, lines, traps, bait – all to no avail. He was mystified. The people of the area hunted crocodiles and considered them a wonderful delicacy. They also had pigs – but no fish.

Passed down from generation to generation, however, were stories of huge creatures that lived in the lake. They had even been caught on occasion by their ancestors. Over the years the talk had escalated into what was a veritable legend.

A Papua New Guinean Loch Ness Monster?

But while the stories of these creatures were related with great seriousness around the village fires at night, like the Loch Ness Monster, this monster was nowhere to be seen.

There were just no fish there, no fish to be caught.

MAF began service to the people of the Western district late in the fifties – and changed their lives!

Wherever possible, airstrips were built adjacent to every mission and government station in the region. But not at Pangoa. Not adjacent, that is. The only place in the vicinity where an airstrip could be constructed was on the other side of the lake. And while the canoe journey was an extra chore, it still meant that the aircraft did away with isolation. Instead of a number of days of boat travel along a river in hot and extremely humid conditions with a large diesel engine pounding away interminably, the Dennises could be at their mission headquarters in a single hour of air travel. An hour of cool, comfortable flight. No more the interminable river journeys, chugging past steamy jungle trailing its tresses into limpid, brown water. Now the forest canopy sped by, like growing broccoli far below, beneath the wings of a Cessna aircraft.

Life was becoming easier at Lake Murray.

But still there were no fish. Until one day – in 1962!

Sitting at breakfast, looking out across the lake through the shutters of their veranda, Keith and Lillian saw a strange and unfamiliar boat making its way towards Pangoa. They knew every government vessel that plied the waters of the rivers and their lake. The boats of the crocodile hunters who visited Lake Murray from time to time were also well known to them. And, of course, they were very familiar with the old, faithful *Maino*. The *Maino's* coming was always a treat for them. It meant the arrival of their long-awaited, all-too-rare order of food. It meant mail. It meant much-needed medical supplies. It meant, best of all, loved friends and visitors.

But this one they did not recognise. And it wasn't sailing on past Pangoa to the government station that had been established a few years before at the top end of the lake. It was actually heading for the little bay alongside the house.

As always, the epitome of hospitality, Keith and Lillian prepared to welcome guests. By the time the visiting boat dropped anchor, Keith was there alongside to invite the travellers in. "Hi there," he shouted. "Glad to see you. Come ashore. My wife has the kettle on."

"Thanks so much. We've come on a fishing survey," the men said. "We'll be around for a week or so and are well able to live comfortably on board. But we'd be delighted to come ashore and have some tea with you."

A fishing survey! Keith almost laughed. *They won't find any fish here*, he thought. *I've fished this lake from east to west and from north to south. I've been at it now for almost twenty years, and like some Galilean fishermen I've read about, I've caught nothing. Apart from a few not-very-tasty catfish.*

"We'll just throw our nets over right here, then we'll be there," they said. "It'll only take a few minutes."

Keith's eyes goggled when he saw their nets. These were not nets for catching fingerlings and garfish. These were six- and eight-inch, professional deep-sea gill nets. Using a small aluminium dinghy, the men soon had them strung out from the stern of the boat, close to a patch of reeds. The line of floating corks with large glass spheres at either end was a new and unique sight at Pangoa.

My little garfish friends will smile at those as they swim on through, Keith thought bemusedly, as he waited for the men to finish their work. *I could think of better ways for the government to spend its money than on this kind of wasteful exercise.* Not wanting to offend, he said nothing. Guests like these were all too rare.

Keith later told me that for the next hour or so, while he and Lillian enjoyed the unexpected company, he was chuckling inside. After all, this was Lake Murray – his lake. His fishless lake! Anything worthwhile in this lake, apart from crocodiles, was only legendary. This was not the open sea. The thought of an ocean-going trawler – for that is what this visiting boat turned out to be – was just too much of a joke.

"Thank you," the visitors said after an enjoyable time together. Keith and Lillian were wonderful hosts, with a fund of marvellous stories. "We'll come back and moor here every night we're in the area." And then to Keith they said, "Bring your canoe and we'll have a look at the nets before we set off for the government station. We need to check in with the patrol officer there."

Keith stood alone in his dugout canoe as the men positioned their dinghy to lift the heavy net. Starting at the far end, they had dragged no more than a few feet of it out of the water when, to Keith's open-mouthed amazement, there was an enormous splash, and into the aluminium dinghy fell a gigantic, thrashing fish!

It was about three feet long and weighed more than twenty pounds.

The fishermen seemed unperturbed, certainly not the least bit surprised, and kept on with their job. Soon there was another and another of these magnificent fish flapping around in the bottom of the boat.

About five yards away, standing in his small canoe, was a

goggle-eyed, totally stunned, speechless New Zealander! He just could not believe what he was seeing. These fish, these incredible fish, were being caught only yards from his house! And for all those years – those frustrating, fruitless years of fishing – he had had absolutely no indication that they were there for the taking.

By the time the net was emptied, the aluminium dinghy was loaded down with hundreds of pounds of prime barramundi.

For that is what they were. These were not just grown-up garfish. These were the best of the best, served for the pleasure and delight of discriminating diners in the most expensive restaurants of Australia.

"Would you like one for supper?" the fisherman said, handing over a fine example. They had smiled as they had seen Keith's unbelieving and astonished face. "Here, why don't you take them all? We'll keep a couple for our tests. Give the rest to the people."

Always the great storyteller, Keith later told me that for weeks he was troubled by a recurring dream. "I dreamed every night that I was standing beside a huge pile of fish, as high as a multi-storeyed building. They were the fish that I hadn't caught over all those years."

The men who came that day were scientists as well as fishermen, and they set out to determine exactly why those remarkable adult barramundi would never take a hook or lure. But it remained a mystery. Barramundi were everywhere, not only in the area around Pangoa. Lake Murray was filled with them. They are known to be a brackish water fish and usually live around the tropical coastline at the estuaries of freshwater rivers; yet, amazingly, here they were living and thriving in the totally fresh water of Lake Murray, more than a hundred and fifty miles from the coast.

More astonishingly, these fishermen-scientists also caught

varieties of fish that previously had not been known to live in fresh water or even in brackish water. They caught large sea bream and even salt-water sharks in the fresh waters of Lake Murray.

The government trawler and its crew were in Lake Murray for two weeks. They recorded their finds and associated data and then departed. Keith and Lillian Dennis waved farewell from the beautiful sandy beach at Pangoa.

They were left with many happy memories. They were left with another treasure – one of the nets the fishermen had used. "It's yours, now," they were told.

And so the people in the region had an added source of protein, a great new source of food.

Soon, the aircraft of MAF provided a way of sharing the enormous advantage of this new fishing project far and wide. No more did isolated mission and government staff have to supplement jungle food with only canned food shipped upriver on the *Maino* or flown in from the coast. In the past, my colleagues and I had flown literally tons of heavy cartons of canned meat, fish and vegetables across those swampy wastelands.

A new era had begun. And that's how I became a fish merchant.

For Keith and Lillian Dennis to put aside their busy mission work to fish and attend to the nets was out of the question. It was a time-consuming business, particularly after another long gill-net was imported and permanently set on the other side of the lake close to the airstrip. So I would land early in the morning to meet a national worker, take the canoe that was there by the shore, and motor out to the net. I would have the first pick of the catch. Sometimes my order for the day would be for only a few fish that would be thrown on top of a load of cargo already on board bound for another station. On other occasions I would fill the empty plane with fish and set off for the highlands – a giant flying sardine can! My arrival always caused great excitement.

But there is more to this fine fishing tale. For the Lake Murray 'Loch Ness Monster' indeed revealed itself to be far more than just a myth.

How do I know this?

Because one day I caught the monster.

We were in the canoe, and the national helper and I were pulling in the net, retrieving the expected barramundi. As we worked our way along the floating corks, the net got heavier and heavier. The thought that we may have caught a crocodile was disturbing. Trapped, a crocodile would roll over and over, creating extensive tears and tangles in the net. It would have to be taken out of the water for several days to be repaired.

As we strained to drag it in, peering hard into the clear, black water to identify what had been caught, the first thing I saw was a round, staring eye, appearing to look right at me! But this was no crocodile. The eye was brown and about two inches in diameter. I had no idea what sort of monster it was as we slowly heaved it to the surface.

To our astonishment, about ten or twelve feet beyond where my companion was standing – balancing himself in the canoe and straining to keep a grip on the net – we saw a huge tail breaking the surface! Then a large fin – and the awesome, brown, immense body of a fish, the likes of which neither of us had ever seen before.

This was no grown-up garfish. It was a sawfish. Not a swordfish, with a single, clean pointed nose. But a sawfish, with a long snout from which protruded, every few inches, sharp and dangerous-looking external teeth.

Having brought him to the surface, we decided to measure him. We cut a notch in the side of the canoe where his nose 'started' and another where his tail 'ended'. He was seventeen feet, six inches long. He had died, caught in that nylon prison. It was impossible to lift this monster into the canoe so we cut him away and let his lifeless carcass go. He must have weighed a ton. It was a record catch. And as far as I know, my Papua New Guinean friend and I still hold that record for the biggest fish ever caught in the inland waters of Papua New Guinea.

Before we cast him adrift, I hacked off his three-foot-six-inch snout with an axe. My friend took it across the lake to Pangoa where, with formaldehyde from the hospital and some good Papua New Guinean sunshine, it cured quite well. It still makes a wonderful conversation piece, a unique 'show and tell'.

What a fish story Pangoa turned out to be! A story of unknown, hidden treasure; an incredible resource just waiting to be discovered.

There are many great 'fishing' stories in the Gospels. A net so full that it could not be dragged aboard the boat. The coin to be found in a fish's mouth that was used to pay the taxes for Jesus and the disciples. Mending nets, casting nets, catching fish. Fishing stories in abundance.

But this Pangoa story speaks to me of something quite different – of wonderful things that are all around, available to us, if only we know how to find them. This fishing tale is a reminder of the unknown and unclaimed treasures that God has provided for us, perhaps as yet undiscovered.

Often I have heard the cry, "Where is God?" Once, in Portuguese Timor, a man who had spent years on the 'hippie trail', travelling from country to country, said to me, "I've tried everything the world has to offer. I've been everywhere, just wandering. But I think now that what I've been doing these past years is, really, looking for God – but I don't know where to find Him."

Like the fish in 'fish-less' Lake Murray, God is there. He always has been. Greater and more awesome than we could ever imagine. He is available for all who need Him. Spiritual resources are there, all around us. They are there for the taking. But so many people don't even know they exist or simply do not experience for themselves the life that God offers. Many attempt in their own ways to make the most of life. They try all kinds of ways to achieve the best and be most effective. And sometimes, often, they simply give up, concluding, "This is all that life offers me. This is my plateau. This is all there is." And life becomes boringly mediocre.

And many Christians who know something of the spiritual resources that God has provided, who have 'caught a few fish', still live on that plateau of mediocrity. They don't experience the abundance of the spiritual treasures freely available to them.

Yet God has more for us than we can ever imagine, "more than we can ever ask or imagine," He says. There is boundless joy, absolute peace, fulfilment and richness of life – there for the asking, there for the finding.

Have you become accustomed to less than the best?

Maybe you should try another method of fishing!

Have you tried lately?

13

Fun

"I have come that they may have life, and have it to the full."

John 10:10

Yes, there are fish in the lake at Pangoa. Along with other things.

With the advent of MAF service in the area, Pangoa became a popular spot where mission staff went for much needed rest and recuperation. Lake Murray's seemingly unending shoreline of tropical forest and grassland, and its exotic reed-encircled islands, stood in sharp contrast to the heavy, steamy atmosphere of so many other places in the lowlands of western Papua New Guinea. With miles of clear, cool water and a great beach at the mission station, Pangoa was a perfect place for a vacation! And Keith and Lillian Dennis made it more so.

Some miles to the north, at the top end of the lake, a government officer was also stationed at a patrol post. He loved to sail, so he had a beautiful, sixteen-foot racing catamaran shipped out from England. With white, billowing sails, racing across the waves of Lake Murray, his fancy little craft must have raised a few eyebrows among the area's native inhabitants.

Quite generously, he made the catamaran available for vacationing missionaries to enjoy. The times I spent on his sleek vessel remain among the most pleasurable memories of my years in Papua New Guinea. Often, when I was 'overnighting' in the area, Keith Dennis and I would go sailing, sometimes well after dark. With a stiff breeze blowing and the sky ablaze with the vivid colours of a magnificent sunset, to skim along, sitting high on the one hull, well out of the water, with the guy wires singing in the wind was pure ecstasy.

In early 1967, Jo and I took our family there for a vacation. I couldn't wait to share with them the joys of sailing on Lake Murray. On our first evening, Keith and I decided to get up really early next morning and take the three elder boys out on the 'cat' before the water got too choppy. Rob, who was the youngest at that stage, was just a little tyke, barely two, so Jo stayed behind with him. Also, she had been unwell for some days before we left. While we were out enjoying ourselves, she noticed that her eyes and her skin were bright yellow, the colour of a canary. Hepatitis! It was no wonder she had felt so bad.

Later that morning, before she went to bed for the next three months, I carried her out to that fancy catamaran to lie on the net between the hulls so that she could have just one chance, just one, to sail. Lillian, who was a nurse, protested loudly. Jo remembers her calling out, "You guys are crazy," as we pushed off from the shore.

After all, what could be better than sailing on Lake Murray? Except, perhaps, waterskiing. Now *that* would be something to try . . .

The advantage of air service for the Dennises came at a significant personal cost in terms of their time. Pangoa was a centre where cargo shipped on the *Maino* was stored for later trans-shipment by air to outlying stations to the north and north-east. Sometimes I would stay there for a number of days, shuttling freight to these places. Keith would put aside his own teaching and construction work at Pangoa to spend many hours working at the airstrip, weighing and arranging cargo loads and helping to load the aircraft.

Announcing my day's schedule on the mission radio every morning, I would give an estimated time of arrival for each airstrip. To make sure that I was not kept waiting at Pangoa, Keith would usually leave home in his outboard-powered canoe at least an hour before that ETA. Bad weather along my route, or even a mechanical fault with the plane, would from time to time delay my arrival and sometimes even force me to cancel the flight at the last moment. That would leave Keith waiting at the airstrip. Always wanting to please and anxious not to hold up the day's flying schedule, he would sometimes wait there for half a day. But he always gave me a joyful welcome when I arrived, no matter how late I happened to be, no matter how much time he had wasted waiting.

Nevertheless, those fruitless hours, willingly given by this dear man, concerned me. Keith and Lillian had an incredibly effective ministry among the people of Lake Murray. It seemed to me that every wasted hour he spent waiting for me was an hour of service stolen from the people.

Back in Sydney, my brother Fred had always had a power boat of some kind or another. Many were my memories of fun-filled waterskiing excursions on a river or in a bay in Sydney's picturesque environs. So I decided to write to Fred and suggest to him that there was something better to do with his latest boat. He didn't hesitate, immediately writing back to say that he would donate a boat to Keith Dennis by selling his own and purchasing a more suitable one for Pangoa.

What a great day it was when the faithful old *Maino* arrived at Pangoa with a new dinghy in tow! It was a smart little thing for those days. All aluminium, with a covered bow, a curved windscreen, and full steering gear. This was no dugout canoe! And what a difference it would make! Keith could now stay on the job at the Pangoa station until he heard the sound of the plane approaching. Then he could crank up the new boat and virtually be at the airstrip by the time I had landed. That little runabout saved hours and hours of valuable time.

And of course, it was fast! And therefore a boat with all sorts of interesting potential. What's more, Lake Murray was big. Big enough for waterskiing!

So the next week, when I was at Daru I sought out the resident crocodile hunter. "George," I said, "you've told me many times how helpful and friendly the Dennises are to you when you go to Pangoa. You say that they will never accept payment for the many times they have given you hospitality." He nodded agreement, and I continued. "You know how hard they work up there, and what they do for the people. I've an idea." He was already interested.

"Did you know they have a new little runabout? How about you trying to lay your hands on some waterskis and some rope? About fifty yards should do the trick. You could have them flown out from Port Moresby. When I'm down here next, I'll grab them. Keith and Lillian could really have some fun! What do you reckon?"

He grinned. "No worries, mate!"

As I taxied into the parking bay at Daru the following week, leaning up against the small tin shed, Daru's 'terminal building', were two shiny new waterskis and a coil of nylon cord! George wasn't there. He had set out on another hunting trip. But he had been as good as his word.

That week, Lake Murray became a resort. Barramundi fishing, sailing and waterskiing. Mission life!

It didn't seem to matter that we shared the water with crocodiles, the occasional salt-water shark and even huge sawfish. They just had to move over. When the flying schedule made it more convenient to overnight at Pangoa, rather than sit in the boat all the way across the lake to the house, I would ski there and back!

And that was only the beginning!

One day, we needed to make a rendezvous with the *Maino* in the river to the south of the lake. We were to pick up a part for a sawmill engine, which I then had to deliver to an airstrip in the north. The *Maino* was still many hours away from Pangoa, so we decided to take the dinghy down there, meet the boat, and pick up the engine part. "Why don't you ski down?" Barry Hadlow, Keith's mission colleague, said. Sounded like a good idea to me!

Barry was a crazy driver and on the way, in a series of imaginative manoeuvres, did his best to dislodge me. And, just once, he succeeded. As we passed a pretty little sandy beach on one of the many islands in the lake, on the outside of the wake and in a screaming turn, I lost balance.

In typically sardonic fashion, Barry turned the boat briefly to check that I was okay and then sped off. "See you on the way back, mate!" he called. Kept buoyant by the life jacket I was wearing, I floated in the deep water, hoping as the minutes ticked by that he really was only kidding. Time passed. But after five minutes or so, bobbing around in the murky brown water, alone, I began to wonder. And grew a little anxious. After all, what else might there be in these waters? Were there teeth that contemplated nibbling my toes?

In time, sadistically calculated, my friend returned.

On the way back to Pangoa about an hour later we passed that same sandy beach. There, basking in the sun, was a fifteen-foot crocodile. I looked with an ashen face at the huge creature. Where, precisely, had he been when I was in the water?

Barry thought it was a huge joke. "There are too many fat barramundi in the water for him to worry about eating a skinny coot like you!" he said. I declined his suggestion that I ski the rest of the way back.

Late one afternoon Barry was driving the boat across to the airstrip to meet me. Keith, fifty feet behind, was skimming across the water, thoroughly enjoying Barry's attempts to dislodge him and send him headfirst into the murky, predator-inhabited depths. Crouched down at the circumference of a wide arc and travelling at great speed, a patterned wake of water flying from his skis, with a huge splash, and guffaws of laughter from Barry, Keith tumbled over and over and finally came to rest upright in the water, unhurt – but minus his teeth!

His empty mouth was wide open in horror, as both top and bottom dentures drifted lazily to the bottom of the lake. A toothless man in such a remote place. Now, that was a challenge, even for a resourceful person like Keith.

When I arrived a short time later, I was told about this somewhat unusual dilemma. I didn't know whether to laugh or cry. It was hard to express sympathy, with Barry in the background grinning like a Cheshire cat, his own teeth still firmly encased in his gums. What were we going to do?

There was an easy solution. I was planning to go to Wewak the very next day. Keith could easily come with me and consult with the excellent dental mechanic at the Catholic mission in Wewak.

But UFM had a firm policy that staff could not travel away from their station without permission. So that evening, to save Keith the embarrassment of announcing his problem to the entire mission community on the radio the next morning, I talked to the field director, George Sexton, and got his ready approval for Keith to make the flight. They were great friends.

George was a colourful character with a dry British sense of humour, and he was not going to let Keith off the hook quite so easily.

"Pangoa, this is Wasua," was the first call on the mission's thirty-minute radio schedule early the next morning. "What's all this about Keith needing some kind of emergency trip to Wewak today?" I can just imagine the conversation around dozens of radios that morning. "That's Mr Sexton's voice. He's hardly ever on the radio. Must be some kind of genuine emergency at Pangoa!"

The ensuing exchange was cruel indeed. For Keith! But for all the other mission staff, spread across hundreds of miles, it was a riot!

"He needs to see the dentist there, Mr Sexton," came Lillian's response, "and Max says it's convenient to take him today."

"Put him on the radio, Lillian. I can't believe he'd want to go all that way just for a toothache," George insisted, feigning ignorance.

"Well, . . . er . . . it's more than a toothache, Mr Sexton."

"Put him on," insisted George. "I want to ask him about it."

So, over the radio, for all to hear, was heard the struggling voice of Keith Dennis – minus his teeth. Almost inaudibly, and trying desperately to articulate normally, came the words, "I fink you know what my problem ish, Chorge. Max shed he'd tell you about it. So, letch get dis ofer wif."

But this was too good a chance for George to make some mileage out of his friend's misfortune.

"Say again? What's the problem, Keith?"

"I need a new shet of denchers."

"A new set, Keith?" queried George. "Why on earth a new set? What happened to your old ones?"

"I losht my teeth, Chorge," was the reticent, humiliated response.

His director was relentless. "How did you lose them, Keith?" he inquired.

The listening radio audience of a hundred mission staff scattered far and wide was thoroughly enjoying the break in routine transmission. It seemed to me the whole country must have been laughing.

"Any suggestions from other stations?" George asked. This was cruel in the extreme.

Suddenly the radio was jammed with a variety of innovative ideas. The first reply came from a station a hundred and fifty miles away, somewhere in the highlands.

"Get a couple of lengths of downpipe, Keith! Put some clear plastic over the end. You may be able to spot 'em with that."

Then the dour voice of Dick Donaldson broke the airwaves.

"Hey, Keith. Tie a piece of meat on twenty-five feet of string," he said. "Then sail slowly over the place where you fell off. You never know, they might snap at that!"

In my imagination, I could almost hear the echoes of laughter from all over the country.

One by one, provocative solutions were delivered. There was no option for Keith but to endure the humiliation. That day, he flew with me to Wewak. Two days later we returned, Keith sporting a flashing new smile and an entirely recrafted reputation!

People sometimes think the Christian life is dull.

I remember a renowned English preacher who, on concluding a summer teaching commitment at our church in Australia, said as his final word to us, "This time tomorrow I'll be on my way back to England. I've had a great time with you. As I go, let this be the word I leave you with: I commend to you the life of faith, the life of following Jesus. It is so much fun!"

There is much joy – full joy – and fun in following Jesus.

Sharks, sawfish, crocodile – all manner of teeth lurk in the depths of Lake Murray.

14

Perfect Pitch

*[I am] confident of this, that he who began a good work
in you will carry it on to completion.*

Philippians 1:6

Was that a piano?

I couldn't believe it! Not here. Not on Daru.

It was unceremoniously lying on its side, on top of a heap
of junk on the back of a garbage truck. Decrepit and geriatric,
this was obviously its last hurrah.

But it was a piano nevertheless.

I was standing by the town jetty, speaking with the district
commissioner about some flights he had requested. It was
1963. Daru was a frontier town on an island off the coast
of western Papua New Guinea. It was the district's administrative and trading centre. Jo and I lived just sixty miles
away at Wasua, a peaceful mission station on the Fly River.
There was no other aircraft based in the entire area, so MAF
willingly made its service available to the government as
well as to the mission.

"Surely that isn't a piano," I said incredulously as the truck
rumbled by.

"Yep . . . sure is. Only one in town; 'fact, only one in the
western district."

"Where'd it come from?" I asked.

"Don't know," he shrugged. "Been here since before the war. In the bar at the club. Had a fair dinkum hammering in all those years, I expect. Given up the ghost now, though. Had it. Totally stuffed."

I raced over to the road and hailed the Papua New Guinean truck driver.

"Hey! Hang on a minute," I yelled. The truck rolled to a stop.

"Wait here a second, mate" I said. I ran back to the commissioner.

"Can I have it?" I panted. "Don't dump it. It's a piano! My wife would kill for a piano."

"Max! It's rotten inside!" the commissioner said. "Termites have eaten away the board that holds all the wires. It's finished, man. It's junk!"

"I don't care!" I said. "Its condition doesn't matter! We might be able to make it work. Maybe it's redeemable! You can put it on the next boat going up the Fly! They can drop it off at Wasua for me!"

He shook his head. He clearly thought I was a nut. But he had the authority to let me have it. He walked over and reluctantly told the truck driver to take the old relic to the government store rather than to the dump.

And it was that simple. We now owned a piano! A second one, in fact.

We had been living in Papua New Guinea for two years, most of the time in Wewak on the north coast. There was only one piano in the town, so a year after our arrival, although we realised that it would probably end its days there, we decided that we would ship Jo's piano from Australia. Life was not really life without a piano. Hers had been a wedding gift from her Gran.

What a day it had been when our 'first' piano had arrived

in late 1962. In those days, there was no wharf at Wewak, and the ship, which came every six weeks from Australia to supply the town, was unable to dock. So an ex-World War II landing barge, owned by the town stevedore, would chug out to where the ship anchored about a half-mile off the coast. The Wewak cargo was lowered into the barge using huge, heavy rope nets. This vessel was something to behold. Its dark orange coat was not the result of a fine paint job. It simply bore the colour of the rust that threatened to consume it. How it stayed afloat was a mystery.

The arrival of the supply ship was always an event. It brought frozen meat, fruit, vegetables, and all kinds of goods to restock the trade stores. Very occasionally it even brought ice cream, the most prized delicacy of all. Only the early birds were able to buy that particular luxury. It lasted a day. Most of the town went down to the beach to witness the unloading procedure. The children would leap into the sea and swim out to where the ships were anchored in the deep bay. You could hear them from the shore all day, laughing and splashing and yelling at the merchant seamen. As the years went by, our four older boys inevitably joined them. They can still tread water for hours.

Jo was down there the entire day when her piano finally arrived. She would have been out on the barge to supervise, had she been allowed, but those rough-and-ready stevedores wouldn't have her on that leaky old barge. So she waited, staring impatiently from the beach, as load after load of the town's cargo made the perilous journey to the shore. Then, at the end of the day – it was piano time.

From a distance, across the water, we watched with bated breath as the treasured crate gradually emerged, cocooned in rope, to dangle high above the hold. Slowly it was lowered into the rusty open relic. Miracle of miracles, it was neither dropped into the sea (as was the fate of many pieces of freight) nor even damaged. Carefully, we drove it home on MAF's old blue truck and lovingly removed the piano from its wooden box. It was just as she remembered it.

Jo spent the next day tuning it. How she revelled in that piano! For three weeks.

Then we were unexpectedly reassigned to Wasua. We couldn't get it there on a DC-3. The airstrip was way too short. So she left her beloved piano in Wewak.

Eventually it was flown to the highlands, where Christian Radio Missionary Fellowship used it for many years in their school of the air. Every now and then we'd tune in and hear Gran's piano crackling over the airwaves.

But now we had another piano!

Unlike Gran's grand instrument, this was not an elegant piece of furniture. Sitting atop the dump truck, it looked decidedly forlorn. Once perfectly lacquered, its wood surface was now laced with thousands of tiny cracks. The lid bore a strange tattoo of small round white circles, where countless wet beer glasses had left their mark. I didn't dare to look inside.

"You wait till the next boat comes. I've got something fantastic on it for you!" I announced to Jo when I arrived home. And a week or two later our second piano, in all its glory, was delivered. This time Jo simply stood there, incredulous.

There were peals of laughter from the gathered crowd as twenty of the village men hauled the old instrument up the steep, slippery river bank. It was placed on a wooden sled behind the mission tractor and dragged the few hundred yards along the airstrip to our house. Then it was manhandled up the lengthy flight of stairs to our open veranda. They didn't seem to exercise a great deal of care.

"Now, let's look inside," Jo said, and gingerly levered back the lid.

Clearly, Papua New Guinean termites had rarely tasted fine German timber. For there they were, happily feasting still.

Originally, all one hundred and ninety-nine pins had been set into a solid wooden plank. But now it looked more like honeycomb than wood. It had been 'aerated' by thousands of hungry creatures. It was paper thin, and had long since shed most of the pins into which the strings had been fitted. Below, in the bowels of this amazing instrument, was a mess of entwined wires, looking remarkably similar to the entanglements that surround a military foxhole.

Amazingly, the dowels and felt-tipped hammers were in reasonable shape. And while many of the keys had parted with their ivory covers, they too were quite good. I guess the termites hadn't got around to them yet. They were enjoying the plank too much.

As we closed the lid, we looked at each other. "We have one heck of a challenge to make this thing even look good, let alone play!" she commented bemusedly.

But this was Wasua! There was no television. No entertainment. We had plenty of time!

So we set about this 'evening restoration' project with romantic vigour.

The first thing we needed was a new plank. Large trees were plentiful in the forests around Lake Murray, with hardwoods, softwoods, and fine, exotic tropical timbers. And there was a sawmill at Pangoa, where our friend Keith Dennis lived. Following my precise measurements, he selected a beautiful piece of hardwood that had been drying under his house for three years. He ran it through his saw, cut it to exact size, and soon had the surface shining. I flew it back to Wasua on the backload of a cargo flight.

Jo already had her piano-tuning equipment with her, and so the job began!

A thousand little white creatures decided with alacrity to

depart the scene as I squirted insecticide over the honeycomb plank and shut the lid down tight. The fact that they probably marched immediately into the bush-timbers of our home didn't really matter to us. There were plenty of 'locals' there anyway. Perhaps the ensuing battle would lower the population already working on the house!

The plank wasn't at all heavy when I unbolted it and gingerly lifted it out of the frame a few days later. It weighed about a pound and a half and was as fragile as a wafer. But it had to be used as a template to position the one hundred and ninety-nine holes in the new plank. This one weighed about a hundred pounds! As we disassembled our magnificent instrument, we organised all the pieces in cardboard cartons on the floor.

The internal organs of a piano are something to behold when all laid in rows. There were exquisite little dowels of different lengths and diameters, as well as keys, hammers, leather joints, tiny little pins, pieces of felt, and pieces of metal. And then there were wires, miles of them, twisted and rusty, all in a heap. It was amazing! And thoroughly daunting.

The mission at Wasua had only an old, twelve-watt diesel generator that pounded, wheezed and gasped for a few hours every evening to provide enough electricity to run a few lights. The use of even a power drill was out of the question. So the preparation of the plank was a long and demanding job. Not only did we need to ensure that all one hundred and ninety-nine holes were correctly drilled, they could not be a fraction wider in diameter than was required. Each had to be straight and absolutely vertical. I'm sure I turned the handle of my drill a million times.

Each threaded pin then had to be carefully inserted to ensure that when wire was attached and the tuning process underway, the pin would slowly wind its way into the wood.

Finally, when we bolted the plank into the frame – it fitted! And it looked great!

Next came the demanding task of sorting out the strings. Each one had to find its correct place in the fixture at the bottom and the adjustable pin at the top. The thick bass strings were more easily positioned. The finer wires of the upper register were the greater challenge, especially as they overlaid each other in groups.

And so this gargantuan task proceeded. From the Wasua village there was a constant rotation of spectators. Not being able to produce a sound yet, this unusual brown box was still a mystery to them. The fact that the pilot and his wife were working so hard on a great mess of strange things must have been the source of hours of conversation around the fires at night. Word spread to surrounding villages, and from time to time unfamiliar faces peered over the veranda. I suppose it was worth paddling a canoe a few miles or walking a day or so through the jungle to see this weird ritual.

Hour after hour, week after week, piece by piece, we laboured on. At one point we joked about whether our furlough, planned for the next year, would have to be put off. But finally it began to take shape again, as a piano. The plank was firmly in place, as were the pins, the strings, the keys and the hammer mechanism.

And at the end, amazingly, there were no parts left over!

Now, for the tuning! Out came the chromed tuning hammer and paps wedges. One by one, I began to turn the pins. Slowly the wires tightened. First a centre string, then a bass string, then a treble, and so on, in rotation, so that uniform tension was applied the entire length of the plank. Night after night it continued, half-turn by half-turn. All one hundred and ninety-nine strings grew more taut by the day.

This was the tedious part of the project. I was sorely tempted to double the pace at which I was tightening them. But we didn't think that would be wise. It was becoming clear that the tension on the plank was going to be enormous. In fact, the total weight to which we were so blithely subjecting our tropical hardwood plank would be in excess of twenty tons. We didn't know this, however, and what we lacked in mathematical acumen, we were soon to discover in a memorable and dramatic way.

After a week or so of this, our piano could just about make a recognisable sound! The villagers were amazed. "Ah-ha, ah-ha," they said to each other, with nods of new understanding. Now they knew! There were smiles all round.

Jo, who was pregnant with Jonathon, was badly in need of a break. So she, Timothy and Michael went to Pangoa for a week of rest. This was my opportunity! I would surprise her! I would have this beast singing like a Steinway by the time she returned! So on a day when rain put a stop to my flying, out came the tuning fork.

I recalled Jo cracking it against the rail of the veranda wall and holding it up to her ear to get the primary tone . . . A440. With a flourish, I did the same and then struck the piano's 'A' key to see how the two notes compared. They were not even close! I checked to make sure I had played the right note . . . the white one north of the two black ones, in the group of three. Yes. Definitely the A.

Bummer!

So I set to work again, cranking up all the strings to what I presumed to be their correct tension and pitch.

When Jo returned, it was finished . . . I thought! With pride, I called her out to the veranda. "Hey, Jo! Now! Just listen to this!"

I sat down and played her the one piece in my own somewhat limited repertoire, "Who Can Cheer the Heart like Jesus." In A-flat. I finished with a flourish, and turned to her triumphantly.

"Great, eh?"

But her face said it all.

"I can't play that!" she exclaimed, horrified. "It's an octave too low! I'll have to sit a foot to the right!"

I couldn't believe it! It sounded just fine to me. Although I must admit, "Who Can Cheer the Heart . . . " had sounded a little melancholy. I argued, but in vain. I don't have perfect pitch, like Jo.

It was back to work again, cranking and twisting on those already stressed-out wires. I winced with every turn, wondering about the strength of Keith Dennis's plank. But we were getting closer. There was joyful anticipation of the days ahead, and a house filled with music again.

Just a few more turns . . . just one or two . . . almost right . . . the days passed.

One evening, having just about reached our acoustic goal, we went off to bed.

It was a classic Wasua night – still and quiet. Often on serene evenings like that, we would lie there and ask each other, "Can you hear anything?" The tiniest sound was discernable; an insect in the long grass on the other side of the airstrip, a dog's bark from the far end of the nearby village, a solitary cricket. Often, as on this evening, there was total silence.

Hours later, it happened.

"Whatever was that?" Jo asked, sitting up. I awoke with a start.

"Whatever was what?" I said. "Go to sleep. It's late."

"Shh! Listen!" she said.

I strained to hear. From the direction of the veranda emanated a most unusual, groaning creak. It was rather like the sound one might have heard on an old sailing ship. There it was again!

I too sat up.

Again!

"Ccrrrrkkkk. Crrrrkkkk" – louder and louder.

And then, all of a sudden, there was a horrendous 'crack'. An explosion that split the night.

We leapt out of bed. The kids woke up crying. The village dogs began to bark.

Within seconds the house was filled with a cacophony of weird, almost musical reverberations.

"Oh no!" we shouted together. "Not our piano!"

We grabbed the flashlight, ran to the veranda, and shone the beam in its direction.

The piano looked normal. It was in the same place. It appeared intact.

Where had that incredible noise come from?

We approached it slowly.

"Max," Jo whispered. "Be careful! Maybe something's trapped in there!" We often had visitors from the jungle take up refuge in our home. Cautiously I opened the lid and peered inside.

There they were. Many of them still moving, unwinding like worms in a box. And the dying strains of some surreal sonata emanated from its destroyed bowels.

I had seen this before. Months before. There was the familiar mess of wires, back again, lying haphazardly over the hammer mechanism. The piano was giving its final performance.

We watched and listened, audience to the death throes of a great old instrument.

Within minutes the Pangoa plank was split from end to end, splintered into a thousand pieces. Pointed fingers of pink wood were everywhere. Some of the pins were still firmly in place but most were lying bare, wire still attached, unwinding.

We began to laugh. All those months of work! Hundreds and hundreds of hours of loving attention. All for nothing!

Next morning, the same men who had carried it up the stairs to the veranda were co-opted once again, only this time to drop the case and its twisted contents unceremoniously over the balcony, where it smashed on to the hard ground ten feet below. Gazing down upon the heap of shattered wood, we thought about the German artisans who, so long ago, had fashioned all the pieces of dowelling, the finely shaped hammers, dampers and other delicate pieces. We imagined how lovingly they must have fitted them all together to create this fine musical instrument.

We kept a few of the strings for odd jobs around the house. It was high-quality wire. The rest we gave to the villagers. All the other metal parts were thrown away.

And the fine German timber? It had the most glorious end. We fed it, piece by piece, through the wood-burning stove in the kitchen. Day after day it yielded its remains to my trusty tomahawk – to become fuel for our cooking. Jo made many a loaf of bread with the heat it produced. What better kindling could one ever find than a hundred-year-old length of quarter-inch dowelling, even if it did have a felt hammer attached to its end?

We had worked so hard at reconstructing that old instrument. We were determined to redeem it. To make it play again. But it never did. Our expectations of beautiful music were dashed to pieces, like that hardwood plank, in a single shattering instant.

And we chuckle every time we think about it.

But there is, nevertheless, wonderful music in our memories of Wasua.

Admittedly, it is not the remembered strains of an old, amateurishly-repaired German piano, but the music of laughter in the voices of those Papua New Guinean people, the harmony of their singing, and the joyful sounds of children playing underneath our house.

Yes, there were frustrated expectations of Chopin, Beethoven and Bach. There was disappointment and a sense of wasted effort. But that is life! Someone once said that the mark of a man's maturity is his ability to cope with frustrated expectations.

But there were expectations that were gloriously fulfilled in other areas of life. We were there less than two years, but we remember it as a time of great happiness and reward as we saw the difference MAF's work made in people's lives. And we both look back with great joy to the many opportunities of personal ministry. Especially for Jo, in the lives of the women of the village.

By the way, God is a master craftsman. He loves to rebuild broken lives. He can untangle the twisted, rusty strings of people's lives and fit them into a new and indestructible base. He will take broken pieces and worn-out keys and fashion them into a wonderful new instrument.

And ultimately, He never fails.

15

The Compassionate Cannibal

Jesus sent him away, saying, "Return home and tell how much God has done for you."

Luke 8:38–39

Amusep would climb into the front seat of my Cessna without the slightest hesitation. He was a seasoned traveller – at least in small Cessna aircraft.

Amusep loved to fly!

Perhaps he enjoyed flying so much because he had walked the cloud-enshrouded mountain trails of his homeland since childhood. You only needed to get a glimpse of his bare, calloused feet, gnarled and scarred, to know they had carried him over many a rocky ridge and covered countless miles of that brutal mountain country. Perhaps as he gazed down upon the mountain trails from his airborne high vantage point, he realised that every minute in the air represented hours of hard, high-altitude mountain trekking.

As a man of the mountains, Amusep was also accustomed to violent weather. He was familiar with the threat of a rapidly developing thunderstorm as it marched across the mountains, filling a highland valley with dense, grey clouds as though poured from a giant, heavenly container.

Which is why, I suppose, it didn't seem to perturb him

when one day, shortly after take-off, billowing dark clouds surrounded the tiny aircraft, and raindrops began snaking their way up the windscreen.

Conditions like this worried most other passengers, but not Amusep. This was simply the way we travelled.

He had greater things on his mind.

He was on a mission.

The mark of God was upon Amusep. He knew that his task in life was God-given. He was one of Papua New Guinea's 'barefoot evangelists', driven by a strong personal passion. And the plane? Simply an aid to his task. It projected him into a degree of usefulness that would otherwise have been totally unattainable. To fly across the mountaintops and over the deep valleys at a hundred and twenty knots when the alternative was a snail-paced, gruelling hike was a miracle to him.

This small, slim, but muscular highlander was a man at peace with his Maker. He loved his people and wanted to share this peace with each and every one of them. The isolated villages of the West Sepik region were his parish, the people of those villages the targets of his deep concern.

This was no foreign missionary. Amusep could never be labelled an intrusive outsider. Rather, this was a man who understood. For the culture of the people was his culture too. He knew their fears. He could identify the spirits that lurked in wait for them in the rainforest and stalked them in the dark of night. He grieved over every sickness that so quickly robbed them of life. He understood the things that bound them.

But Amusep was a man who had found freedom. Freedom in Jesus Christ. To him, freedom had not destroyed his culture, but had breathed life into it. Fulfilment and security had replaced anxiety and fear. Light had replaced darkness. Amusep could enjoy the beauty of the night without fear.

He knew the intertribal rivalries and the animosity that

created intense pressure. He well knew the 'payback' principle that meant no one was safe or secure. He understood the vice grip of evil and treachery that gave little pleasure to the people. And yet he was a man of pleasure, of laughter and of peace. He had a passion to tell his people that the change had come to him through Jesus.

He knew, also, the heart-wrenching sadness that pervaded the entire society because of the lack of healthcare. It took an awful toll. The infant mortality rate was a cultural tragedy, and Amusep knew what could be done about it.

To me, Amusep was a tremendous source of information. He taught me about the various tribal groups and of the very firm boundaries between them. He spoke of the response of the people to the message he carried with so much fervour. Though physically just a small man, Amusep was a man of great stature. And while not all were prepared to accept his message immediately, he loved them still. And he always returned to teach more of the Good News he carried.

Because Amusep worked with the Baptist Mission, I had assumed that he had found his faith in Jesus through them. They had recognised his natural leadership ability and trained him well for work in evangelism, healthcare and education. He was quite an orator, an excellent interpreter, a marvellous teacher, a persuader of men . . .

The sky grew dark and threatening as I flew that afternoon. I took off from Telefomin, the centre of the Baptist Mission work, to Mianmin, in Amusep's home valley. I was carrying supplies to a team of translators working there and was planning to bring Amusep back to Telefomin. When I landed he greeted me with his familiar grin and, after quickly helping me unload the aircraft, climbed aboard for the return flight. He too had been watching the threatening sky and knew that I would be in a hurry.

Once airborne, we talked about the best way to negotiate our way back through the valleys. There was no chance of out-climbing the rapidly deteriorating weather. We flew west down the Mianmin valley, trying to find a way under the clouds, following the river into the higher mountains, towards Telefomin. All the while the weather closed in. It was like flying through a tunnel whose floor, heavily timbered, serrated and rocky, was as threatening as the dark clouds above.

I knew one of the airstrips in the area was available as an alternative. And we could always return to Mianmin. But the thought of spending a wet and cold night there made me persevere just a little bit longer. There was simply no way through. Black clouds completely filled the valley system ahead and behind. To the left and right, reaching thousands of feet above, clouds were 'filled with rocks and trees.'

'Roughing it' was going to be the order for the night.

I turned to the left into the narrow entry of another valley, Eliptamin, and soon had the airstrip there in sight. I made a quick circuit and advised the Civil Aviation controller that our intention was to land and stay overnight.

It was beginning to rain by the time my trusty Cessna was parked at the top end.

Amusep was out of the plane in an instant, saying as he darted off into the trees, *"Mi painim ples bilong slip bipo ren i cam wasim yumi."* ("I'll find a place for us to sleep before the rain comes and drenches us both.") It was raining heavily up towards the Eliptamin village, some distance away. The track was enshrouded with cloud.

The lean-to shelter the mission had built there was soon completely rainproof, thanks to my industrious friend. He had gathered armfuls of a soft fern upon which we would sleep. Marvellous bushman that he was, he very quickly had a large pile of dry firewood safely out of the rain's way and a warm fire burning. I took a few emergency supplies from the aircraft while Amusep ventured off into the forest again, returning with some sweet potato that was soon roasting at the edge of the open fire.

The sweet potato looked like charcoal on the outside, but underneath its black crust it was delicious. Huddled in the darkness beneath a crude shelter beside the fire, we enjoyed a great meal. Soon we were lying down, listening to the consistent pattering of the rain on our leafy roof.

Amusep asked me about my earlier life, my home. I told him about my wife and children at Wewak, about my own childhood. I talked of my schooling and my boyhood passion to fly. And I told how I came to Jesus, of the feelings of peace and security that had brought to me.

"What about you?" I asked him. "How did you become a follower of Christ? Was it at Telefomin, through the Baptist missionaries?" He grinned. I think he knew what my reaction was going to be as he told me his story.

"I came to know Jesus when I was in prison," he said.

Prison! He had got my attention!

"I was taken to the coast with a number of other men from around here." He gestured with his hand. "We spent ten years locked away there."

In his wonderfully expressive pidgin language he went on, "Some of the other Mianmin men and I killed the first government officers to come into this territory. We ate their bodies. We ate also the bodies of some of their carriers whom we had also killed. But other white men who came searching for their lost friends hunted us. We were caught, taken to court, and sent to prison on the coast. It was in prison, the *kalabus*, that I met Jesus!"

Killed . . . and ate?

I'm sure I swallowed nervously. This man, my gentle friend Amusep, had killed and eaten someone. Someone just like me. And here we were, huddled together. Alone. And I had to spend the night on this dark, isolated mountain airstrip alone with this self-confessed cannibal!

Amusep enjoyed my reaction to his tale.

He told me why that tragedy had taken place. The killing and its horrible aftermath had been motivated not so much out of treachery or maliciousness, but out of fear. The Mianmin people had become increasingly apprehensive. A message had been called from ridge to ridge that a group of strange 'spirit figures' had come to the valley to the east and were making their way along the river up towards the Mianmin valley. The members of that early expedition had been totally unaware that their progress along the river valleys was not only being monitored but continually communicated ahead. Thus apprehension among the Mianmin escalated. Day by day their fear grew as these strange creatures came closer and closer.

Perhaps these were the spirits of ancestors coming to wreak some kind of vengeance upon them, they thought. Two of the strangers, it was told, had skins that were not brown but white. And their bodies were covered in a weird, unfamiliar way. Even their feet had some unusual covering.

Fear gripped the people of Mianmin. They had but one alternative. It was well-planned and carefully carried out. These people were masters of ambush. The exploring party had no chance.

That their bodies were ceremonially eaten, simply had to be. It was the fashion – the custom.

There was no pride as Amusep told his story. There was no bitterness about the prison term. Instead, there was gratitude. These primitive mountain men had been taken to the coast and, in prison, had been taught to read, given simple medical knowledge, mechanical training, and an education in life skills. Thus they eventually returned to Mianmin uniquely equipped to contribute to the development of the area.

But the outstanding memory of his time in prison was of the people, brown and white, who had told him about Jesus.

We marvelled together, my friend and I, at the plan of God that had brought us together that night. Two entirely different men, a pilot from Australia and a cannibal-become-pastor from the remote mountains of Papua New Guinea.

Neither of us could fully understand the other's culture. Our languages were different, our homes, our families as well. Amusep certainly had the edge on me in terms of survival skills and bushmanship. But the great central commonality we shared was that each of us had been sought out by God and commissioned to do His work.

The sky cleared, and we prayed together. We were two brothers, worshipping the One who had made the canopy of stars now shining brilliantly above.

I slept well and peacefully that night in the company of this great man from Mianmin. He cared for me so gently, staying awake to tend the fire to keep me warm, watching against any danger that may have lurked there behind us in the forest.

Today, Amusep is in heaven with Jesus. His is a name virtually unknown outside Papua New Guinea. But he played a significant part in the establishment of a living and vibrant church there in the mountains of Papua New Guinea. And his was a name familiar to the Father of Eternity as he was welcomed into heaven.

We will have a joyful reunion one day, Amusep and I.

16

Of Cows, Cans and Communion Wine

OF COWS . . .

Put cows in my plane? Never!

Mine was a special plane. It had a unique role. It carried very important people. Yes, it carried a lot of general cargo as well. But cows? No way!

I wasn't in the cattle transportation business.

I looked after my aircraft meticulously and with loving care. I cleaned it regularly, even polished it from time to time. It wasn't a cattle truck!

Besides, I knew nothing about cows. A boy from the suburbs of Sydney, not the country, I was no cowboy. The closest I came to being a cowboy was at the local movie theatre every Saturday afternoon when my friends and I sat enthralled with the heroic exploits of Roy Rogers and John Wayne.

Every year as kids, we went to the Royal Easter Show in Sydney, and while it was fun to watch the cowboys rope and tie calves at the evening rodeo and wonder at the craziness of men who rode humongous bulls that looked incredibly fierce and dangerous, it was not a world I understood – or even wanted to understand. As I walked through the buildings at the showgrounds where the thoroughbred cattle were on display, I didn't care for the way they glared at me through the horizontal bars of their prison-like stalls. It was obvious they didn't like me. I certainly didn't like them – the way they smelled and especially what they dropped on the floor.

In very truth, I was no cowboy.

Put cows in my plane? Not if it was up to me.

But the request had come from a friend on his remote station a hundred and fifty miles away. "I've arranged to buy a couple of heifers from the Lutheran Agricultural Station near you. They'll be a great help in our agriculture school. Could you please bring them in? Bring them in one at a time. I'll cover the cost."

But it took many weeks to get approval to take the heifers across regional borders, and in those weeks, these two young members of the bovine family ate and ate – and got fatter and fatter! They surely didn't look like heifers to me when I first saw them being driven along the road towards the airstrip. They were full-grown cows to my inexperienced eye. The pride of the Lutheran herd!

With a sense of impending doom I asked the agriculturist who had brought them, "How am I going to get them into the plane? Who's going to help?"

His reply did nothing for my sagging enthusiasm. "I'll help you," he said. "We'll find others to give you a hand." It sounded to me as if I was to be in charge!

I was to learn many lessons about cows that day.

For a start, cows don't lie down just because you want them to. In fact, they strongly resist any effort to make them do so. They resisted absolutely everything I wanted them to do! I was exhausted by the time we had the first one lying on the ground so that it could be tied up with the endless lengths of strong rope I had bought for the occasion.

And by then I smelled just like my reluctant passenger.

The ten or so near-naked mountain warriors, who had been recruited to help as they were walking down the road, lay straddling the cow, thinking this was great fun. To them, this was just another kind of pig – a very big one, a very strong one. Strangely enough, cleanliness and order having long since departed, I was beginning to think it was rather fun as well. The cow was the only one thinking otherwise.

It took a long while to get her into the plane. Bellows of protest during that hour had attracted a veritable crowd of people who now stood around laughing and offering enthusiastic advice. Great entertainment for them. As I sweated and strained, I thought back to those men who roped and tied the calves at the Royal Easter Show. I was glad they weren't watching!

Neither of my passengers would stand on the scales for me, but I guessed they weighed about three hundred and fifty to four hundred pounds each. It was a pretty rough guess. Getting the first cow into the plane had been such a complicated business, and I was such a disgusting mess that the thought of repeating this performance the following day had little appeal. It would be better for me, I decided, though maybe not for the cows, if I threw in the other one as well.

The thought that I might kill two birds, as it were, with the one stone had interesting connotations. Little did I know.

After a couple of hours, all was ready. My unwilling passengers were on board, trussed up with so much rope that it looked as if they had run into a giant spider web. As well as the rope that tied horn to heel and shoulder to shank, I had covered the entire wretched, struggling load with the heavy nylon mesh net that I always used to secure cargo in the plane. Two pairs of eyes, however, revealed something less than a contented state. They glared at me with malevolent stares from within their netting prison. Out of two slobbering mouths came a terrible noise, and what was worse, these two large, brown, hairy creatures had demonstrated their absolute derision and antagonism towards me by depositing a disgusting and horribly smelly mess on the clean floor of my polished Cessna even before I commenced the take-off.

This flight needed no delays, no diversions.

Climbing towards the high pass of the nearby mountains, however, it soon became obvious that my passengers were somehow in cahoots with the weather to take revenge on me. The far peaks were covered in billowing, darkening cloud. It would not be easy to find a way through. I tried hard, very hard, and even harder as I contemplated the prospect of having to land at an intermediate strip somewhere along the route and allowing my passengers to disembark. The thought of overnighting somewhere with them to await better weather the next day . . . was just too much.

There seemed no way through. In absolute frustration I radioed my wife to inquire about the weather back home. At least there were agriculturalists there who could be babysitters. "Don't come back here," Jo advised. "Since you took off the weather has really deteriorated. I don't think you could get back anyway."

Wonderful!

Why did I say I would do this job?

Realising my predicament – for these were very, very smart cows – they began to play their part to make the situation worse. They kicked and jerked, and kicked again, over and over until the plane began to shake, and I became increasingly concerned. If they forced their way out of their leg restraints, their strong legs could surely make a hole through the aircraft or at least do considerable damage.

And worse, if they did struggle free of the ropes and net and try to stand up, there just wouldn't be enough room in the plane for the three of us. We could crash!

And I didn't want to slink sheepishly (!) into heaven, smelling like this!

What a mess . . . in more ways than one. I really didn't know quite what to do.

Then . . . the penny dropped! I had the solution.

I remembered back to my days as a jet-fighter pilot. On every flight I depended on oxygen, as most flights were done above thirty-five thousand feet. I recalled the first day, in 1956, when my cadet class, feeling like guinea pigs, went through various tests in the decompression chamber at the Royal Australian Air Force's School of Aviation Medicine. In an effort to teach us about the dangers of oxygen deprivation, anoxia, half the class would not be provided oxygen as the chamber was 'taken up' to an equivalent of thirty-five thousand feet. The rest of the class breathed oxygen all the way, only taking off their oxygen masks when finally reaching the same altitude. It was a fascinating and salutary lesson to see and feel the different, but sure and deadly effects of anoxia upon the human body.

But these were cows, for heaven's sake!

Nevertheless, they needed to be quietened down. And I needed a few thousand feet of extra altitude to get over the weather.

Making no mention, of course, of the needs of my bovine passengers, I called the Civil Aviation authorities with my intention to climb to at least sixteen thousand feet for a while to get over the weather. Taking the yellow mask from under my seat and turning on the oxygen flow, I began the long climb towards the blue sky I could see above the towering weather.

Amazingly, the cows became quite restful. They settled down to nap for a while!

Keeping a close watch to make sure that their heaving chests remained heaving, I scraped over the lowest section of cloud and, now able to see the low country ahead, began a long, slow descent towards my destination. I wanted it to be slow!

It was with a confident air that I delivered my two passengers to their new owner about forty minutes later. With a little help from some of his friends, we were easily able to unload them. They were drowsy and docile, so glad their journey was over.

As they were led off along the jungle track towards the meadow that was to be their new home, they turned around to look at me, one last time. Their brown eyes were soft and tranquil – a little sleepy, it seemed.

I think they quite liked me!

I think God was smiling.

OF CANS . . .

I did some stupid things in aircraft when I was young. I remember looking death in the face more than once flying a jet fighter, and if I had died on any of those occasions, it would have been totally my own fault. I was only twenty years old.

In my MAF years I remember only one occasion when death seemed at hand. It wasn't during take-off or landing – which made it even more unexpected. It was while cruising in a clear blue sky on a very routine flight . . .

The MAF warehouse at Wewak was always full of freight and supplies. As quickly as we flew them out to the four corners of the country, the merchants and shipping agents in the seaport town where we lived would bring more in.

Every morning our client missions would make requests on the radio regarding things that were most needed from the cargo bay where their supplies were stored. The mailbag was always the top priority. Usually after mail came the frozen food stored in the large freezer in the hangar. After these specially requested items were weighed and manifested, it was simply a matter of trying to lower the pile of stuff that remained.

My load for the flight on this particular day was fairly typical. I had been into Wewak for maintenance on my plane and was heading home. En route I planned to drop most of my cargo at a mission station near Wapenamanda where we lived. There was mail. There were fresh vegetables, cartons and drums of canned food, educational and medical supplies. Everything was individually weighed and marked, then listed on the manifest. Very routine.

The national workers at Wewak were very good at loading the plane. They had worked for MAF for many years and knew exactly how to ensure that the aircraft's centre of gravity was within prescribed limits. The plane was fuelled for the planned time of the flight plus the required sixty minutes of reserve. A phone call to the Civil Aviation authorities assured that the flight plan was in order. The aircraft was in good shape. The cargo load was within limits and correctly stowed and restrained. I climbed up on the wing strut to check personally that the fuel contents were as I had requested and that the tank caps were securely closed. Ready to go.

As I climbed aboard I felt confident that nothing had been neglected; however, I did notice that the load was bulky. It filled the entire cabin . . . but that was not unusual. I tried to move some of the cargo stowed right at shoulder level behind the pilot's seat, but it was too firmly restrained, so I squeezed my way around it, sat down and began to run through the pre-start checklist and get the flight under way.

Take-off and climb-out were uneventful. The weather was great. I could see the mountains a hundred miles away. I had an hour and a half to go, and the prospect was for a very normal flight. Probably a little boring.

From ten thousand feet the Sepik River looked like a huge wandering serpent as it curled its way through the region. Motorised canoes left their V-wakes on its brown surface.

The ground was freckled with the shadows of the light fair-weather tufts of cloud at about five thousand feet. I checked my position and my time to the river. On time. On track. Jo had told me on the radio that the weather at Wapenamanda was also clear, so it seemed like a flight that would be uneventful and soon forgotten.

Very routine. Yes, rather boring.

Then, in a split second . . . there was an incredible explosion. The noise was literally deafening.

Everything went white. There was no instrument panel, no cargo, no aircraft, no view of the river or the mountains, no cloud. Inside, outside, above and below – everything was white. Disorientation began to set in. I felt as if I could not breathe. I didn't know where I was.

My first thought was that I had been involved in a mid-air collision, that there had been an almighty impact there at ten thousand feet over the Sepik River. But I could see no red fire as my aircraft burned, no pall of black smoke. There was no heat, no light, no pain. Everything remained – just white. And totally quiet. I was enveloped, entombed in a dense, white silent cloud, and I felt strangely, unusually, comfortable.

This must be heaven. So this is what it is really like, I immediately thought. But I sensed that I was fully conscious, and I wondered, *What on earth is happening to me?*

I have no idea how much time passed before, from the impenetrable nothingness in front of me, a dim, surreal impression of a ghostly white instrument panel began to appear, coming slowly into focus. And as the strange whiteness began to move about in front of my eyes, I could see that the air speed was still at its correct one hundred and twenty knots, the altimeter still read ten thousand feet, and the turn-and-balance instrument was indicating that the plane was flying straight and level.

I peered ahead, confused, dazed. Then gradually I became aware of something else. It was the faint noise of the aircraft's engine. Slowly it got louder and louder – until I could hear it quite clearly. And it sounded absolutely normal. In fact, everything was normal – at least as far as the plane was concerned.

But a strange feeling of dryness gagged in my throat and nostrils.

What happened? What had happened to me?

By now, I could see my two hands appearing out of the whiteness. They were still on the control wheel holding the aircraft straight and level.

I looked down at my arms, my legs and my thighs.

Aha . . . I had the answer.

On each of my legs and arms was a ridge of . . . pure white flour! Like tiny avalanches in tiny snowy mountains, flour was falling to the floor as I moved. The peaks of the flour crests were about three inches high, right along my legs and arms. I shook my right hand, and the air in front of me, which had begun to clear, was once again filled with a cloud of flour blowing around like a minute snowstorm.

I smiled, then laughed loudly, almost hysterical with relief, as I realised what had happened.

I wasn't in heaven. I hadn't gone suddenly, in a catastrophic crash, to meet my Maker.

Turning around, I saw the evidence. A strong, steel can holding twenty-two pounds of flour that had been wedged just behind my right shoulder had burst apart in an explosive failure. It was ripped apart from top to bottom along the seam. Pressure differential had found a fault in the can's manufacture, causing a huge, instantaneous explosive decompression. And in that split second, twenty-two pounds of fine white powder had been atomised, discharged with tremendous pressure into the restricted space of that fully loaded aircraft cabin. The noise had temporarily deafened me. The flour was everywhere, filling my mouth, my ears and my nostrils.

I slid down in the seat to catch my reflection in the glass of the instrument panel, and sure enough, I had a cone of white flour, reaching almost to the roof, on my head. Small rivulets of flour ran down through my eyebrows at the front and under the collar of my shirt at the back, giving me extra padding against the seat. No wonder I had felt so comfortable.

Thinking that I should fly straight home instead of to my planned destination, I stayed as 'still as a mouse' so as not to disturb my hilarious appearance. I flew the plane ever so gently down into our home valley and did as smooth a landing as I could. I wanted Jo to see what it would be like to be married to the abominable snowman or, at least, to see me in this hysterically funny state, hair and eyebrows whitened in some kind of premature ageing, dressed in ghostly white clothing, and wearing a cone-shaped hat of flour on my head.

Did I hear a heavenly chuckle?

OF COMMUNION WINE . . .

It was hot in the noonday sun at Madang – very hot. One didn't need an atlas to confirm that we weren't far from the equator. The air was so humid. This was doldrums time – there was not even a suspicion of breeze.

Loading the plane in the heat that day, I looked as if someone had squirted me with a hose or I had fallen in the ocean. And either would have been welcome.

The demanding task of loading a huge, very heavy wooden cask of wine into the Cessna wasn't helping either. I could see people laughing at me, passengers walking across the tarmac to board a couple of old DC-3s, the workhorse of Papua New Guinea's development in those days. *Look at that crazy guy*, they must have thought, *dripping with sweat, rolling a gigantic keg across an airport tarmac!*

Why couldn't the Lutherans use grape juice in nice small cans for Communion wine like most other people? I thought to myself. *Why does it have to be the genuine article, shipped all the way from Germany? And if they wanted this stuff, couldn't they buy it in bottles rather than in this ridiculous, enormous barrel? Why had I drawn the short straw to have had to come down here in this sticky, stinking heat to pick it up?*

The thought of that straw – be it short or long – came to mind again later in the day.

They were great friends, these Lutherans. We so much enjoyed living on their base at Wapenamanda. Flying for them was always fun . . . and very rewarding. But they were different. I thought about my upbringing. Not a drop of alcohol had ever crossed the lips of my dad or my mum. We had been brought up to believe that one taste of the forbidden strong drink would certainly land us on the threshold of Hades! Our Lutheran friends thought somewhat differently. No grape juice for them at Communion. Only genuine, best-quality port wine would suffice. The real stuff. From a faraway German vineyard.

So here I was, struggling to get this ancient wooden monster containing fifty gallons of the stuff across the tarmac. I had no idea how I was going to get the keg into the aircraft, to lift it the three feet up over the sill of the door. I knew it would have to be carried lying down. It would not fit standing up.

It took quite a while, a number of people, and two large lengths of timber before the barrel was finally rolled aboard. The rest of my cargo was loaded around and on top of it.

The cool air through the vent system was a welcome relief as I climbed out of Madang towards the mountains. The worst of the exercise was over. There would be plenty of help to unload this item of sinfulness. But as I looked ahead I realised that perhaps the worst wasn't over. In the couple of hours I had spent on the ground at Madang the weather had deteriorated markedly. The horizon had changed from the serrated blue-black beauty of the mountain range into the crisp white outline of developing cumulonimbus clouds. *I certainly won't be able to get through there at ten thousand feet,* I thought.

It wasn't too bad, however. I found myself skimming the tops of cloud at about thirteen thousand feet, and a call to Jo at home told me that the weather was quite fine at Wapenamanda. With the background of the smooth-running Continental engine and listening to the chatter on the radio, I felt quite relaxed. My shirt was dry again. At last I was cool. This was my final flight for the day. All was well.

Suddenly, there was a loud, sharp sound, almost like a rifle shot.

Whatever was that? I looked around at the full load of cargo behind me. Nothing appeared to have moved.

But then I heard – and smelt – the answer. Both at the same time.

The noise was – 'Glug . . . glug . . . glug . . . glug.'

The smell was – sweet, enticing, intoxicating!

That huge wooden cask with its fifty gallons of prized port wine, all the way from Germany, was slowly emptying itself into my aircraft. The bung had failed, flying like a bullet to the back of the plane.

And I could do nothing about it.

I couldn't pull over to the side of the road and block the hole. I couldn't call upon the services of a load master or another crew member to stand it up and stop it from emptying itself all through my Cessna.

I could do nothing – so I simply kept going.

It suddenly crossed my mind that if this stuff, this dreaded product of a faraway vineyard, really tasted as good as it smelt, my family had missed out on all kinds of great things all those years. Maybe we hadn't been so smart!

The picture of what my plane might look like to those on the ground was quite intriguing. No Cessna like mine flies high enough to make a condensation trail high in the sky as does a high-flying jet airliner from time to time. But this was no condensation trail of freezing water vapour. After all, any airline pilot could make one of those. This was different. I was making history here, laying down a condensation trail – and a red one at that . . . of prized German wine.

It was quite sad to think that no one appreciated this wondrous phenomenon.

I don't know whether one can get drunk on the smell of wine, but I thought about that, too.

As I considered the situation, it occurred to me that my ignorance of the nature of wine casks had contributed, at least in part, to my present predicament. I knew nothing about anything to do with wine. Had I known more I would have recognised the necessity to load the keg with the bung at the top. Then, I suppose, I may have had only a few gallons of wine in the plane . . . a few more when I lowered the nose to descend. But in my ignorance I had rolled the barrel in with its bung at the bottom, and I had the whole nine yards – no, the whole fifty gallons – of that entrancing-smelling stuff sloshing around in the bowels of my plane.

As I eventually lowered the nose to descend, I could hear it swishing around, finding its way to the front, wetting the heels of my shoes. By this time I was beginning to think about the awesome amount of work this wretched, now-empty keg had created for me. It was going to be a major task to clean the aircraft. I might have been an ignoramus in the ways of wine, but I knew that it would be terribly corrosive if not totally washed out or otherwise removed.

At the thought of what MAF's chief engineer was going to

say to me, or maybe do to me, I grimaced. Not only was he almost paranoid about us keeping our aircraft in pristine condition, he was even more an ultra-conservative teetotaller than I. *Would he see the funny side of this?*

I wondered. He wouldn't.

He didn't!

After landing at Wapenamanda, I carefully inspected my aromatic aircraft. There was a beautiful, glistening, purple-looking sheen all along the underside of the rear fuselage. Yes, indeed, I must have laid a glorious trail across the blue mountain sky.

I smiled as I wondered whether minute droplets of this wonderfully-smelling brew would have reached the ground, penetrating the heavy forest below. Maybe some primitive hunter caught that aroma and set off at a run to find its source.

Needing a respite from the smell – from the whole, hilarious episode – I drove home to have lunch before I commenced the long task of cleaning up. It would mean taking all the panels out of the floor and washing every single piece of metal, every cable, every pulley. I needed to have a break first. Besides, I wanted to tell Jo all about it.

As I arrived home, my next-door neighbour, the pathologist at the mission hospital, was in his front yard. I couldn't help but tell him about the episode before I went inside.

"You mean to tell me that there were fifty gallons of that wonderful stuff washing about in the bowels of your plane?"

"Not only that, John," I replied. "There are gallons of it still there in the cargo pod under the plane."

My friend, John, a colourful character from southern USA, turned around towards his house, cupped his hands to his mouth, and yelled, "Honey . . . get the drinkin' straws. We're goin' to the airport!"

I'm glad God has such a great sense of humour.

17

Extreme Sport

But those who hope in the LORD will renew their strength.
They will soar on wings like eagles.

Isaiah 40:31

Question: How do you get a downed aircraft out of a river bed deep in a remote South Pacific jungle and have it flying again in less than a week?

Answer: With great difficulty, a lot of help, and heaps of fun along the way!

There was the usual early-morning chatter on the radio. Pilots were giving departure, position and landing reports and requesting weather and traffic updates. The flight service officers were answering questions and passing on other necessary information. It was 'operations normal' on this early morning in September 1966. The day's flying was getting underway. The air was full of talk! Aircraft all over the country were feeling their way through the clearing fog and haze of a typical tropical highland day. Then –

"Mayday, Mayday, Mayday . . . "

There is no other cry, no other call, that so demands instant attention and concern in the world of aviation. The response is immediate. All other communication ceases.

And so it was on this day.

"Mayday, Mayday, Mayday, this is Bravo Victor Kilo." It was one of our MAF planes. "Position, Yuat Gap, over the river at nine thousand feet, descending. Total engine failure." Pilots everywhere held their breath. The call continued.

"My intention is to attempt a forced landing on the river bank at the northern end of the gap."

Land on the bank of the river in the Yuat Gap? It couldn't be done. I knew that area well. There was no river bank there at all that could be in any way used to land an aircraft. Although the river was running lower than usual, any exposed bank would be steep and muddy or a mass of huge, round rocks. You simply could not land a Cessna 185 there!

Bravo Victor Kilo (BVK) had departed from its base at Wapenamanda only twenty minutes earlier, at 7:00am, bound for Wewak on the North Coast. The Yuat Gap was a familiar place, an en-route reporting point. There, the high mountains part, forming a broad canyon through which the turbulent waters of the Yuat River force their way before eventually emerging from the high country to flow on down to the lowlands.

Immediately, aircraft began diverting to the area. To everyone's astonishment, within minutes another call from Allan, the pilot. "Madang, this is Bravo Victor Kilo. Safely on the ground on the east bank of the Yuat River. The aircraft is only slightly damaged."

Safely on the ground? Only slight damage? Surely it wasn't possible.

But it was soon confirmed. Circling aircraft could see Allan waving from the rocky area where he had landed.

MAF's PNG Field Leader, Max Flavel, and I were over the site by 8:30. We could hardly believe what we saw. There, in the centre of a narrow strip of large, white rocks, was BVK. The aircraft appeared totally intact. Allan, as reported, was standing nearby, waving. I descended, made a tight circle just above tree level, and flew low along the river to see exactly how and where he had managed to land.

In the sunlight, framed on one side by thick jungle and on the other by the swiftly running river, the rugged little Cessna looked strangely out of place.

Soon, a full-scale rescue operation was underway. A government-chartered helicopter was already en route to the Yuat Gap. The priority was always to get the pilot out quickly. Max and I flew to the nearest airstrip at Biwat, a small Catholic mission station midway between the forced landing site and the Sepik River. We had arranged for the helicopter to take Allan there. Within minutes he arrived, having left BVK to the mercy of a rising river.

Huddled around an office table in Wewak that evening, we made our plans. We could not abandon this valuable aircraft there. It absolutely could not be lost. Its work was too important!

From Allan's report of the damage, we calculated that, apart from changing the engine, a day's work, it would only need an hour or so of repairs to make it flyable again.

But there were no heavy-lift helicopters available in Papua New Guinea at the time. Removal by river was the only way. And time was of the essence. In those parts, an exposed river bed never lasted long. One good night of rain would raise the water level, and faithful old BVK would be washed away.

The decision was made. A most extraordinary recovery mission would be attempted.

It was a full Cessna that landed back at Biwat at 8:00am the following morning. Our 'rescue' party consisted of Ray, an MAF mechanic, Allan, BVK's pilot, and myself. Basic food and camping supplies for a few days and a heavy aircraft toolkit made up the remainder of the load.

The priest at Biwat was very helpful. He took us in his small motor launch as far as the water conditions would allow, to a riverside village called Sipisipi. It was a slow and laborious trip upriver.

Sipisipi was a most pleasant place. The people there treated us royally, unused to so many 'foreign' visitors. As we drank the milk of fresh, sweet coconuts, negotiations commenced. We wanted three canoes and, we thought, about ten men. Clearly, this was no ordinary day in the life of Sipisipi. Every man, woman and child in the village wanted to come. We eventually settled on twenty-one able-bodied men. Our village friends insisted we would need at least that many. After all, who would haul the canoes through the rapids?

Rapids? I shifted uneasily.

Two of the canoes were about forty feet in length, the other a little smaller. They sat low in the water, weighed down with food, gasoline, tools and supplies. Barely six inches of rough wooden hull remained above the water line. It was precarious in the extreme. Gingerly, I lowered myself into my canoe. *"Sindaun. Yu no ken wokabaut. Maski sanap."* ("Sit down. Don't move around. Don't stand up.") I happily obliged. There were jaws in the waters below! Hungry jaws! I had no intention of falling in. Our Sipisipi friends showed no concern whatsoever. I began to wonder whether this plan of ours was going to work. But when all was ready, our little recovery party set off.

For the remainder of that day, like intrepid explorers breaching the unknown wilderness, we crawled upriver. It was a circuitous route. The only noise was the incessant howl of three single-cylinder Archimedes outboard motors. Where in the world they came from and how they kept going remains a mystery to this day. Pieces of wire, hand-woven cord, an amazing assortment of tools, and spare parts wrapped in a dirty old cloth were on hand for any emergency. But, amazingly, those mechanical marvels ran on, howling hour after hour, their exposed little flywheels spinning crazily in the boiling sun.

As we progressed, the river became narrower and narrower – and faster and faster. In the shallower sections we could see a rough, rocky bottom. We were approaching the white-water rapids. But by this time I had become convinced this venture might well be nothing more than a foolhardy dream. Here we were, struggling upstream in canoes that seemed barely afloat.

Soon we would be returning, *with an aircraft on board!*

The procedure for negotiating the rapids was simple. Air Force pilots would call it 'line astern', one canoe behind the other – with a considerable distance between them. Then, heading to the place with the least amount of 'white', each driver in turn would commence the assault. Completely disregarding the welfare of his little Archimedes motor, he would plunge into the rapids at full throttle.

Inevitably, however, when there was no more headway to be made, we would await the call, *"Olgeta kalap na godaun, na supim kanu!"* ("Everyone over the side and push the canoe!")

This was mountain water and very cold. But a wonderful relief from roasting in the sun.

Trying to find a foothold on the slippery rocks below was tricky enough. But manhandling a heavy wooden canoe through the rapids was difficult in the extreme. We took many a ducking, the rushing water flooding over our heads. Most of the time we just clung on, hoping that at least one or more of our crew had his feet planted firmly on the slick bottom. Then, having safely navigated an area of white-water rapid, we would all clamber on board again, soaking wet and exhausted, and motor on to the next challenge. Sometimes it lay only a hundred yards ahead.

The day was long, laborious and exhausting. Rapid after rapid after rapid. I clearly recall that, at one point, looking back after hours of struggling, we could still see the place where we had stopped for a break earlier that day. It was about half a mile downstream.

But what fun.

Towards evening, different shades of colour in the water indicated that we were approaching the junction with another river. As we reached the mouth of the Maramuni, a river familiar to us from the air, we looked for a spot to camp. Just as the light was beginning to fade, we found a place that would do. It was not ideal, but it was all that was available. There was nothing there but jungle, water, mud and a very small patch of somewhat level, hard clay where all twenty-four of us would be bedding down for the night.

Allan, Ray and I were very weary. But the men from Sipisipi were still excited about this new adventure. It didn't take them long to unpack the canoes and make a fire.

Our meal of canned meat and rice was augmented by taro, sago and bananas – the staple diet of our companions.

Before I went to sleep, I remember looking up into the black velvety sky and wondering whether the stars could possibly appear quite so bright from any other place on earth. They were like pinpricks in the floor of heaven. I marvelled and worshipped the God who made it all.

I had not been asleep for more than a few minutes when I was rudely awakened. I was roughly shaken by two or three men who looked at me with staring, concerned eyes.

"*Yu no ken slip. Taim yu slip, nus bilong yu em i krai. Dispela krai i olsem krai bilong puk puk man. Sapos puk puk meri em i harim yu, em i kam. Sapos i painim mipela, em i kros na kaikai mipela!*" ("We can't let you sleep. When you sleep, your nose makes a noise like the male crocodile. When the female hears that cry, she will come and, instead of finding a mate, will find us here. She will be very cross. She will eat us!")

Now, my wife Jo has never been particularly fond of my snoring. Indeed, quite the contrary. But according to my new Sipisipi friends, a female crocodile would find it irresistible.

So they took shifts to ensure that I didn't sleep all night, or at least not deeply enough to allow the sound of my gentle breathing to escalate into its inevitable raucous snore. They told me I could catch up on sleep during the next day. Sure. In a cabin cruiser! But these canoes were not cabin cruisers.

At sunrise the next morning I was up with the rest of them, anxious to be on our way. With Archimedes howling, we sailed off for another day of pushing and pulling, slipping and sliding, sitting and swimming, dunking and near-death experiences.

I think we were the pioneers of 'extreme sport'. And this was 'Tarzan' country. Today people pay a small fortune to do what we were doing.

But then came an unexpected challenge. We had noticed that our Sipisipi men had become more and more subdued as the day went by. They talked quietly among themselves and called out from canoe to canoe in their own language. By mid-morning, they disclosed what was worrying them. They didn't want to go any further.

"Em i taim mipela go bek long ples. Mi ting mipela inap long painim balus pinis long hia. Mipela no ken walkabaut moa." ("It's time we went back home. We thought we would have found the plane by now. We can't go any farther than this.")

They explained that we had long since reached and passed the limits of their traditional territory. They said that our progress would have already been monitored by unknown tribespeople, fierce and warlike men who would be very unhappy that we were invading their area. They were afraid we would all be killed.

It took much talking to persuade them to change their minds. We explained that from the air we had never seen any villages further upriver than Sipisipi. And besides, we knew we weren't far from our destination. We could see hazy blue mountains ahead. In river miles, of course, we had no idea how much farther we had to go. It was a solemn crew that reluctantly continued.

Another tiring day. On a number of occasions a propeller struck a rock, shearing off the cotter pin and sending the motor into a screeching howl. Yet again, it was into the water. While repairs were made we struggled to hang on and prevent our trusty vessel from being carried away, out of control, backwards!

Finally, as evening was drawing near, our little convoy of three rounded a bend. And there it was, about a quarter of a mile ahead. Our yellow and black Cessna sat, with a certain air of dignity, on an exposed bank of huge white rocks.

Bellows of exultation reverberated up and down the river valley. We had made it!

Ray and I were absolutely astonished. In spite of its resting place, BVK was virtually undamaged. There was not even a black rubber mark on the stones. Just a flat tyre and very slight damage to the tailplane. As chief pilot, I was impressed. What an incredible landing!

Our Sipisipi companions were not so happy. Clearly nervous and agitated, they didn't want to stay. They believed there were enemy tribes all around us and, also, that there was not enough food for them to eat. We had to do something to restore their confidence, to persuade them that they would be fine. We told them it would not take long at all to disassemble the aircraft and be on the way back downriver with it.

But they were not easily convinced.

As an encouragement to them and to reassure them that

we were not really at the end of the world as they feared, we called the Wewak base on our portable radio and requested that they arrange an airdrop of rice and tinned fish in the morning. The provision of this extra food supply would be advantageous as well as an incentive for our helpers to stay.

The men insisted that they mount guard on our camp that night in case of attack by marauding cannibals. Ray, Allan and I were too weary to be concerned about such things. Obviously, I had not had my promised sleep in the canoe during the day. Thankfully, my national companions were most preoccupied. Female crocodiles were less worrisome than hungry cannibals. I slept like a log.

With the dawn came a lessening of tension. We had made it through the night without being attacked. Soon after, we heard the welcome sound of our airborne room service approaching. The Cessna from Wewak flew low overhead. The Sipisipi men were ecstatic. The right-hand door had been removed and they could clearly see the piled bags of food stacked on the door sill. Following a couple of very low runs along the river, and just at the most propitious moment, the bags were pushed out and came raining down, right on our stony beach. Nearby, BVK sat awaiting disassembly.

The airdrop worked wonders for our transport crew. They thought it was amazing. These white men had talked into a little black box late in the afternoon saying ridiculous things about fish and rice. Then, the next morning, fish and rice had come tumbling down from the heavens.

As the men had brought a shotgun with them, we had asked that a few packets of extra shotgun cartridges be included in the sacks of food. Soon our crew had someone continuously out hunting. By the time we were ready for our return trip a quantity of meat – pig, cassowary and smaller birds – had been caught and was being smoked in a quickly made smokehouse.

The task at hand was no small feat. First, engine and wings were removed. Planning the loading of BVK in readiness for the trip downriver took quite some time. We decided to connect the two larger canoes together, somewhat like a catamaran. Then our twenty-one strong men lifted the aircraft off the stones, carried it to the water's edge, and positioned it with one main wheel towards the front of each canoe. We made a simple wooden frame between the two canoes, near the stern, for the tailwheel. It was not necessary to lash them together. They were securely held by the weight of the plane. One wing was placed beside the fuselage. The engine and the other wing were placed in the third canoe.

This unorthodox rescue craft looked weird, to say the least, but the weight of the aircraft was evenly distributed and it seemed to ride well in the water.

Had Papua New Guinean canoes ever held such a load? I think not.

The water at our rocky beach was running fast. About five hundred yards downstream it increased in speed to become a bubbling white rapid, the first of many before becoming a smooth-flowing river. After much cogitating, we decided that until we reached those smooth waters below the area of rapids, the only way to ensure control with such a top-heavy load was to drive the canoes under power upriver against the current. Then, by reducing the throttle, we would allow the craft to drift in a slow, controlled manner down-stream – backwards!

We were all nervous. But the time came. It was now or never. We piled on board, taking our allocated positions, and cranked up the ever-faithful Archimedes. With the prow of each canoe heading upstream, we worked our way to the middle of the river and held our strange flotilla motionless against the current. Then, reducing the power, we began our forward-facing, backwards trip home!

It worked!

The two canoes, firmly connected and now sitting lower in the water, were quite stable, providing a much more comfortable ride for us 'white skins'. We could actually sit safely on the side of the hull, and even stand up and move about.

As we approached the first rapid, more throttle was applied to counteract the increasing speed of the river. Backing, then, into the white water, the outboard motors strained to compensate for the increased current. So, as before, it was *"olgeta kalap, na godaun."* Everyone over the side again, to manhandle our strange contraption, inch by inch, through the rapid to the smoother, deeper water.

Following each stretch of white water, we would rest in the calmer sections. If necessary, we baled out the canoes.

And so it went on. Rapid after rapid.

Only once did we almost lose our 'ship'. Perhaps the water was too deep or the rocky river bed too slippery. I don't know. But suddenly, at one point, we found ourselves being swept away, broadside and out of control. Frantically, we grabbed on to any parts of the hull we could reach, and clung on desperately. Like a crippled bird, our wingless yellow Cessna almost became the 'Yellow Submarine'. It was a wild ride! We were a waterlogged lot, spluttering and coughing, when finally we shot out into calmer water. Carefully we fished around and retrieved the bailing equipment, an assortment of half-coconut shells, cans and scoops. As quickly as we dared, we emptied out the hulls before climbing back in.

As we progressed downstream, to our relief, the rapids eventually became less frequent, and we were able to return to travelling in a conventional fashion – facing forwards.

Exuberant yells of triumph were shouted from the canoes as we approached Sipisipi. There were looks of open-mouthed astonishment from the people on the shore when they saw our amazing little flotilla sail past their village. We were nearly home safe!

And finally, there it was – Biwat.

Then my heart sank.

Because of the low water level, the river bank at Biwat was an almost vertical wall of slippery, terracotta-coloured clay, about twenty feet high. It marked the airstrip threshold. I barely managed to scale it on all fours. Standing on the grass at the top, I wondered how on earth we could ever lift the plane up to the airstrip. I began to wonder if it would be better to take our strange convoy the extra day or so downstream to the larger Sepik River, and there find an easier place to bring the plane ashore.

I shouted down to the men in pidgin.

"Listen! Please, listen."

They looked up with enthusiastic boyish grins. I barked my orders. "Do not do anything," I said. "We are not going to lose this aircraft. Not now! Not after all this effort. You are to wait where you are. We're going to have a walk around to see whether there is a way up here." I had an awful vision of the entire contraption tipping over before my eyes and the tail of BVK slipping ignominiously beneath the waters. I was determined not to allow this precious aircraft to end up at the bottom of the river.

But our Sipisipi friends had other ideas.

In Papua New Guinea there are many strange sounds. But there is no mistaking the sound of a group of men at work. The only way I can describe it is as a series of great, rhythmic, corporate grunts. It is the product of enormous joint effort. And while Ray, Allan and I were walking along the airstrip, to my horror we heard it. We turned. There, like a golden phoenix, from the kunai grass at the end of the airstrip, rose Bravo Victor Kilo.

Incredibly, the men of Sipisipi had simply walked up that

almost perpendicular, slippery wall with an aircraft on their shoulders! And deposited it on the ground at Biwat.

All done. Their job was finished!

To this day I have absolutely no idea how they accomplished it.

Then the celebrations began. Hollering and whooping, they grabbed the plane, and lifting the tail high into the air on its main wheels, they ran it, backwards, from one end of the airstrip to the other.

And we three foreigners, who had thought mistakenly that we were in charge of this exercise, stood and watched – and smiled! This was their moment. Not ours!

I flew home a few hours later. Ray remained at Biwat to install the replacement engine that had been flown in earlier. Next day, as I was flying some hundred miles to the West, I heard on the radio, "Madang, this is Bravo Victor Kilo, taxiing Biwat for Wewak." Thirty minutes later the invincible BVK, with a new engine and a few temporary repairs, was back in our Wewak hangar. Safe and sound. It bore a decorative coating of Biwat mud – and the hand prints of twenty-one men.

We made a lot of mistakes in our recovery of BVK in 1966. We nearly lost the old thing a couple of times. We ran the risk of leaving a broken, useless airframe in a faraway jungle river. But we put in a lot of effort. We dared to consider the impossible possible. It had to be done. Or at least tried. And it paid off. And this was only an aircraft! A piece of machinery.

The world is littered with broken lives. On the surface they might even appear whole, but like old BVK sitting on a faraway patch of rocks in the jungle, they are dysfunctional, damaged, even lost.

And lives are of infinitely more value than aeroplanes. God cares about them. Every last one of them. He hears each cry for rescue, for redemption. Lost and broken people get his special attention. He will leave ninety-nine who are safe to bring back one that is lost.

That's why Jesus came.

But, unlike our stumbling attempts on the Yuat, God makes no mistakes when He is invited to lift up, repair and rebuild. Nothing is impossible with Him. He loves to redeem, to rescue, to recover.

> *But those who hope in the LORD will renew their strength.*
> *They will soar on wings like eagles.*
>
> Isaiah 40:31

Do you need to be rescued . . . to fly again?

18

The Lostness of the Lost

"Suppose one of you has a hundred sheep and loses one
of them. Does he not leave the ninety-nine in the open
country and go after the lost sheep until he finds it? And
when he finds it, he joyfully puts it on his shoulders and
goes home. Then he calls his friends and neighbours
together and says, 'Rejoice with me; I have found my
lost sheep.'"

Luke 15:4–6

It was the greatest show on earth. But it was no three-ringed circus.

It would have been an international blockbuster, but no Broadway or Hollywood producer could have put this show together. Its cast of tens of thousands was totally untrained. Yet each one knew his role before the show was ever envisaged. There were no rehearsals. There was no programme. There were no lights, no sound system. No tickets. There was not even an audience! The set was magnificent and unique. No artist could ever have painted that mountain backdrop. It was indeed like no other show on earth – ever.

And it was a stunning success!

It was called, simply, the Mount Hagen Show.

It was a gathering together of warriors from the mountains

and valleys of the western and southern highlands of Papua New Guinea. For some years there had been a smaller annual show, or 'sing-sing', at Mount Hagen to which the people of the Whagi and other nearby valleys had been invited. But this year, 1965, tribes from hundreds of miles away had been invited to come as well. From villages and hamlets perched precariously on the sides of steep, spectacular mountains. From faraway valleys. This was to be a coming together of people who had never met, indeed whose awareness and knowledge of each other was very scanty. Most of these men had never seen a town – or a car. They were wild and exotic people. This show was for them and for them alone.

Inviting them to gather at Mount Hagen was a part of the government's strategy to unify a deeply divided people. It was part of the plan to make one nation out of hundreds of different tribal and cultural groups. Seven hundred and fifty languages! A gargantuan task.

To an outsider these men, with their common Melanesian features, may have looked the same, but the subcultures among them were profoundly diverse. Bringing them together might help them see that despite the unique differences between their tribes, they had great and unifying commonalities. This gathering was to facilitate their ultimate unification as one people to take their place among the nations of the world with dignity and pride.

The entire concept was considered by some to be reckless in the extreme, an invitation to riot and debacle. But it was going to be exciting!

By messages shouted from ridge to ridge across that rugged land and carried on foot across the mountains, the word was sent out. "There is going to be a *'bigpela sing-sing'* at Mount Hagen." Boundaries, sacred and sacrosanct, were to be lifted to allow free travel for all, even sworn enemies, to make their way there.

This show was the main topic of conversation all over the highland regions. I was asked about it at every airstrip. Excitement mounted, and a sense of eager anticipation was everywhere.

As the day grew closer, groups of colourful men from faraway valleys began the long walk to Mount Hagen. They marched with pride through 'enemy' territory, challenging any authority who tried to stop this granted free passage. As they walked, they sang a strange chant-like cadence.

Bodies were greased to a bright sheen with pig fat and tree oil. An amazing array of brightly coloured feather head-dresses, made from the dried carcasses of birds of paradise, marked these men as unique among world citizens. The vivid brilliance of these tall, waving crowns of glory was in stark contrast to the charcoal-blackened faces and the circles of white ochre ringing the eyes of the proud wearers.

They held their weapons high, these highland men. And with great pride. Long spears of polished black palm, bows with arrows intricately carved and tipped with wicked-looking sharpened bone. In each bark belt was a traditional stone axe, the blades hewn from mountain rock, patiently and meticulously ground to the traditional shape and sharp edge.

Standing on the porch of our house at Wapenamanda, watching these men pass by on their long walk to Mount Hagen, I pictured thousands of them all in one place at the one time. It was going to be an incredible spectacle, an historic occasion. It was not to be missed. I simply couldn't stay away.

At the last moment I decided to take our second son, three-year-old Tim, with me. It was to be a special day out with Dad for him. It proved to be special in an entirely different way.

We flew the twenty minutes to the Mount Hagen airstrip and walked the mile or so to the large area of level valley land set aside for the show. By the time we arrived, dust was swirling and rising from tens of thousands of feet as these magnificent highlanders leapt and danced their way in a strange circling movement around the arena. Their intriguing singing was, to the uninitiated, more akin to yelling. An unusual cacophony of sound. The air was electric.

As some had predicted, there was a fine line between spectacle and danger. The spears, arrows and stone axes brandished by these fighting men were not toy weapons. These were the weapons of war and of death. These were men of war and of death.

With Tim on my shoulders, I approached the split-bamboo fence roughly erected a few days before and now encircling a solid mass of human bodies. Tim's little knees tightened against my neck. He grasped two fistfuls of my hair, far too tight for comfort. His excitement rapidly became apprehension.

Entering the enclosure we joined the crowd, or more realistically, we were simply absorbed into a maelstrom of people. There was nothing else we could do. It was not a matter of moving around from group to group. The many thousands moved as one, like a massive, brown, human whirlpool, rotating in slow motion. It was impossible to walk against the flow. All around us, shoulder to shoulder, were men, not simply of another culture, but of another age. The smell of sweaty bodies, of tree oil and pig fat was almost overpowering.

The noise was deafening. Every warrior was singing the high-pitched yelling chants unique to his own tribe.

And in the middle of this incredible spectacle, perched high on my shoulders, my small, snowy-haired, pale-skinned boy – dressed so neatly in white overalls and matching hat by his mother for this special day – was very uncomfortable. And increasingly afraid. He was constantly being brushed in the face with feathered headdresses and had to push aside bows, arrows and spears. He cried for me to let him down. I carried him in my arms for a while, but he then found himself bumping not against feathers and weapons but against strong, sweaty, greasy bodies.

It didn't take long to decide that one circuit of that large arena would be enough. This was no place for a little boy.

I tried to stand still but the crowd pressed us on. I lifted Tim down to the ground, and holding his little hand firmly, I tried to work my way to the periphery of the arena.

Perhaps he needed to wipe his eyes; perhaps it was because our hands had become oily and greasy we were pulled apart. I don't know. I just know that, in an instant, his little hand was jerked from mine.

He was gone, lost in that crowd. Danger. Extreme danger. And I could do nothing about it.

I yelled for people to get out of the way to let me find my son. I pushed my way back through the press of brown, gyrating bodies to where we had been when our hands slipped apart. Not finding him, I forced my way forward, then back against that milling crowd – but he was nowhere to be seen. I elbowed my way towards the centre of the circle then back again, yelling his name continually. But it was all to no avail. My voice was lost in the noise of that place. A little boy three feet high was not to be easily seen, nor his voice heard.

Fear, abject fear, exploded throughout my entire being. I had lost my son in that seething mass of humanity, in that hostile and dangerous place. I fell to my knees in an attempt to see him among the impenetrable barrier of dark, dusty, dancing legs, appalled at the thought that he could be so easily trampled underfoot.

Guilt flooded over me. What a stupid and irresponsible thing I had done in bringing him here. I should have never put him down to the ground – or let him go.

176

In this very, very dangerous place I found it hard to control panic.

There was no office to which I could go to report him missing. My frantic shouts drew no attention. Tens of thousands of others were also shouting. Very few could even understand my language or my pleas for help. The occasional English-speaking foreigner who came by could do little but shrug his shoulders. They were sympathetic but soon were forced to pass on. I didn't know whether to move along with the crowd or to remain in one spot.

I felt paralysed with helplessness.

The minutes stretched on. It seemed that for hours I struggled from place to place trying to find someone who could help in my attempts to locate my son. I found one government officer, but there was little he could do.

I cried out, with deep emotion, to God, "Please, please, help me find my son. Please protect him. Please keep him safe in this incredibly dangerous place. Please."

I have no idea of the duration of time of my total despair. Perhaps it was only thirty minutes. It felt like many hours.

With an increasing sense of doom I worked my way to the edge of the crowd. There was rising ground there. I had made a full circle of that vast area. Climbing the flattened grass of that little hill with a heavy, heavy heart, I was physically and emotionally drained, completely exhausted.

But as I walked up the slope, overwhelmed by dejection and loss, I saw a little white boy at the edge of the crowd, standing by the bamboo wall. With him was a Papua New Guinean boy just a few years older.

Tim!

He threw himself into my arms, gripping me with all of his remaining strength. Totally dishevelled, his once clean outfit was brown with dirt and grease, his little white hat long since gone, no doubt by now trampled into a small, unrecognisable piece of dirty ragged cloth. His face was streaked with the dried mud of tears mixed with dust. He buried his head into my neck and, with a hoarse, exhausted voice, sobbed into my ear, "Daddy, Daddy, I was . . . been . . . trying to find you."

I sobbed with him. For several minutes I clung to him as if I would never let him go again. My tears were of indescribable joy, my sobs of deep relief. My precious little son was found. I stood there, profoundly thankful to God for answered prayer.

Only then did I turn to the small Papua New Guinean boy. I looked down at him as he stood there by me with a wide smile on his face – a warrior in miniature. His joy was obvious as he saw the little white-skinned boy he had rescued reunited with his father. His little body shone with fat and oil. He carried his weapons and his little stone axe with pride. His feathers were beautiful, his face blackened with charcoal.

I lifted him with my other arm and held him close, sharing my tears of relief with him. He didn't understand the words of my outpoured feelings of gratitude as I told him over and over again how much I loved him for what he had done. I owed the life of my son to him, but I didn't know how to express it, how to repay him.

Eventually I put him down and, emptying my pockets, gave him all the money I had. It seemed such a paltry reward. He had given up participating in what was to him an unbelievably exciting thing to help a distressed little white boy.

But he soon rushed off into the crowd, and I have never seen him again. I have often wondered what happened to him. Did he grow up to be a proud village warrior? Was he one, who, as development and independence finally came to Papua New Guinea, achieved great things in the leadership of his people? I don't know. But I do know that he meant more to me that day than I could possibly have told him.

I took Tim 'far from that madding crowd.' We finished our special day in relative quietness and arrived home hours earlier than we had anticipated.

The 'lostness of the lost'. What does this mean . . . to you? What does it mean to God?

That day has become for me an unforgettable benchmark against which I regularly and with great seriousness measure my own life. Even today, as I relive the anguish of that hour and then its wonderful conclusion, things come to mind that are of momentous importance.

The analogy, the parable, fails in some respects, but in others it is potent and telling. If, as an imperfect human parent, I could feel the depth of emotion and passion that was mine that day, if 'separation and lostness' produce such an overwhelming sense of love and concern – and if God is truly our Father – how does He feel about the lost of this world?

The Scriptures clearly tell us "your father in heaven is not willing that any of these little ones should be lost."

Jesus, in the parable of the lost sheep, made it abundantly clear that finding His lost children is paramount to the Father. The shepherd's responsibility demands that he leave the ninety-nine to seek and save one that is lost.

A final thought. As I think of that young boy from Papua New Guinea, as I recall my deep love and gratitude to him, I am reminded also of another great and wonderful truth.

The Father has a special measure of love for those who bring the lost back to Him.

19

I Will Take Him from Here

*He tends his flock like a shepherd: He gathers the lambs
in his arms and carries them close to his heart.*

Isaiah 40:11

*Are not five sparrows sold for two pennies? Yet not one of
them is forgotten by God . . . Don't be afraid; you are
worth more than many sparrows.*

Luke 12:6–7

The call on the aircraft's radio caught my immediate attention:

"Bravo Victor Kilo, there is an urgent medical emergency
at Nuku. Can you airlift a male patient to Wewak?"

Flying towards the coast on the return leg of a cargo flight
to the highlands, I was within thirty or so miles of Nuku.
Yes, I could make the diversion. From where I was I could
see the hills to the south of Nuku.

Yes, I could do it . . . but . . .

This had been a busy day, and I was already running behind
schedule. A medical emergency would really mess up the
day. Flights would have to be cancelled or rescheduled to
the already tight programme of the following day.

As I turned away from my homeward track and reduced
power for the descent ahead, frustration took priority over

compassion. I wondered whether the patient really was ill enough to justify this disruption. Too often such flight requests had turned out not to be emergencies at all.

Descending overhead the small government outpost of Nuku in a tight turn, I could see a missionary friend standing at the top of the very steep hillside airstrip, a small human form lying on a stretcher beside him. No one else was there. As I landed and taxied the aircraft to where they were, I saw no movement from the still figure, even in response to the loud noise of the extra engine power needed to climb Nuku's steep airstrip and position the aircraft by the stretcher.

The small boy, perhaps ten or twelve years of age, was gravely ill.

He was also alone. No parent or guardian was there to travel with him.

Compassion took over from frustration, leaving me feeling guilty.

Barely conscious, the boy's startled eyes were filled with fear as I lifted him into the plane and laid him on the floor. There was no seat for him, and the crude stretcher upon which he had been carried to the airstrip could not fit into the aircraft. There was not even a mat to insulate his wasted and feverish body from the cold of the metal floor. The threadbare cloth wound around his thin body did little to help.

His brown face was almost white. Crusted mucus around his mouth and the salt of dried tears around his sunken eyes gave him a ghoulish appearance. But his eyes pierced my heart. They stared at me with a wordless appeal for help and mercy. His physical pain was compounded by fear, the total unknown of being placed in an aircraft.

Terror and pain don't make a pretty face.

I couldn't tighten the cargo straps across his tiny chest. He was too small. As I bent over his little body to secure him as best I could, he made a moaning noise. His eyes closed. I was glad. He would be better off unconscious, I thought. The air was quite turbulent that day.

As I fastened my own seatbelt and readied the plane for take-off, I knew that this was no false emergency. Gone were my concerns about passengers waiting for me on other airstrips. They would understand. This young Papua New Guinean boy needed, and received, all my attention and concern.

Nuku airstrip at that time was no more than a very steep, grass-covered hill. I tried my best to avoid the bumps as the plane accelerated down the slope, but the spring steel undercarriage of the Cessna made it very difficult.

I heard a quickly inhaled breath, and my young passenger winced as his little body was bounced about. I prayed, "Please help me find a smooth path for this kid." As soon as I was airborne, I climbed quickly to cruise at four thousand feet, above the level where the steamy, rising heat from the jungle below created turbulence.

To my departure call I added, "Request an ambulance on arrival. I have a seriously ill stretcher patient on board."

With the aircraft trimmed for the forty-minute flight to the coast, I gave my full attention to my suffering passenger. I reached down and took his limp brown hand in mine. His face was still twisted with that same mixture of pain and fear, but responding to my touch, his eyes opened, slowly at first. He sighed deeply, and his lips moved to an ever so slight, tentative wisp of a smile.

We made a special connection in those moments, that boy and I.

We looked into each other's eyes. There was more than eye contact. Our hands were clasped together, but it was more than simply holding hands. Words weren't necessary, nor were they possible. Our communication was deeper, more profound. It was heart-to-heart, a blending of emotions. Pain was being covered with compassion, fear with love.

He didn't understand the words of my prayer as I prayed for him. But God did.

I knew that if any one of my five little boys at home were in such a precarious position, hundreds of people would pray for his healing. For this boy there was no one – but me. As I pleaded with God on his behalf, for life and for healing, the roaring of the engine may have overwhelmed the sound of my words, but it couldn't overwhelm my passion.

I felt his response. He seemed to marshal the minute amount of his remaining strength. He squeezed my hand. It wasn't strong. But I felt it. It seemed to say, *Thank you. Thank you for making me feel safe. Please don't let me go.* He was not suffering alone.

We flew along in that bare little ambulance that day – holding hands!

I saw his brown eyes soften; I watched his fear begin to melt away. Replaced by calm. From the corners of his dry, cracked lips came a further, very slight movement. His weak smile, though still bearing the marks of pain, broadened. He returned my love. I know he did. His sunken eyes, ringed with that white salt of dried-up tears, were speaking to me, telling me he was glad that I was there.

God had heard and had answered my prayer. An immediate answer. Somehow, as through our hands we were physically connected, I knew that I was the connection, a true and certain connection, between heaven's love and this lonely, needy boy.

The air at that altitude was still, the weather good, requiring that I give only an occasional glance at the instruments and a quick scan of the sky outside. I kept eye contact with my little passenger. As the minutes went by, I spoke with him of God. Of healing. Of trust. As he squeezed my hand with the remnants of his almost depleted strength, I loved that kid as if he were my own.

The world would never know him, or notice – or even care. History would not record his life. He didn't stand tall even in his own village, nor in his nation. He didn't rate a guardian to accompany him to the hospital. Perhaps he was an orphan anyway.

He was just a sick little boy from the jungle. And he captured my heart.

But God also cared, and He had sent me along to be His agent of compassion to this frail, wasted child. This boy, made in the image of God, was of immense value. Many years before, Jesus had said that not one sparrow "will fall to the ground apart from the will of your Father . . . you are worth more than many sparrows." This boy was not going to escape the Father's attention.

And so we flew on.

God answered my prayer for him that day, but not in the way I had so passionately requested. I had prayed that his life would be spared, that a period in the hospital under expert medical care would return him to full health.

A warm peace washed over his face, a face no longer ghoulish but somehow radiant.

I saw his eyes, which never left mine, slowly begin to glaze and lose their sight. They didn't close. His grip slowly lost its meagre strength, and I watched the rhythm of his heaving chest slow down until there was no more movement. The little hand that had gripped mine became softly limp.

I watched that precious little kid die that day – with a smile on his face.

And I cried.

I gently unclasped his lifeless hand and laid it on his now-still chest. I closed his eyes. They bore no more pain.

His body took on a particular dignity, lying there on the cold metal floor.

Something very special happened in that plane as it flew on across the Sepik basin that day. Yes, there was a lifeless body there on the floor beside me. But there was another presence in that bare cabin. A holy presence. I felt it. I felt the presence of angels, almost the brush of their wings, as they came to collect a very precious life and gently carry it away.

My weeping was exchanged for a peculiar joy. I knew that the real life of that young Nuku boy, call it what you will, the soul, the spirit, had been taken through a glorious transition. He had gone through what the psalm describes as 'the valley of the shadow of death'. And I had the priceless honour of holding his hand as he walked through that valley. Another hand took him as he emerged on the other side, a new person with a glorious body.

I turned the aircraft back towards Nuku. I just had to take him home. Trying not to let my emotion show I made a call, "I'm returning to Nuku, estimating there in twenty-five minutes. Please cancel request for an ambulance."

Thousands of years ago a prophet, calling the people to the challenge of declaring who God really is, said:

"Here is your God . . . He tends his flock like a shepherd: He gathers the lambs in his arms and carries them close to his heart."

The God of eternity, the creator of the universe – gathering lambs, giving them the highest priority? For some, that must be the greatest paradox. For others, for me and hopefully for you, it is the most wondrous thing.

God – a loving shepherd? Almost too much to believe!

I saw the Good Shepherd at work that day – in my plane! He gathered that beautiful young boy into His arms and carried him close to His heart. Why? Because a young boy from Nuku is of great value to God, as great a value as any other boy that ever lived!

The blessing was for him, yes, but the blessing was for me as well.

Some may wonder and question, but I am convinced that I will meet my little friend in heaven one day. The experience of that day demands that I believe it. The answer to my prayer was far more than healing for him. It was wholeness. A heavenly, eternal transaction took place in that Cessna plane at four thousand feet above the Sepik jungle. It was not a transaction of words. It was a transaction of Love.

God assigned to me the task of bringing him to the gates of heaven. He then said, "I will take him from here." I will ask him his name when we meet.

20

Thanks but No Thanks

*One of them, when he saw he was healed, came back,
praising God in a loud voice. He threw himself at Jesus'
feet and thanked him . . . Jesus asked, "Were not all ten
cleansed? Where are the other nine?"*

Luke 17:15–17

To feel appreciated is a basic human need.

And a simple 'thank you', easy to say, means so much. To give thanks is more than good manners. It is a gift.

We never lacked for 'thank yous' in mission aviation. Our service was always deeply appreciated by church and mission, and by the community at large. So often we were their lifeline to the outside world, mountain and jungle barriers broken down by our little Cessnas. And gratitude was expressed in wonderful and creative ways. Perhaps it was homemade lemonade and cake served on the tailplane. Just to say thank you.

Sometimes one dear lady, with great care, would drape a white lace tablecloth over the metal surface and artistically arrange morning or afternoon tea, in true British tradition. Bone china cups, delicately made little sandwiches – even a silver teapot! All surrounded by hundreds of near-naked, Stone-Age warriors!

Almost every day we would bring something home from someone. A pawpaw, a bunch of bananas, fresh vegetables, sometimes even strawberries or roses, unknown on the coast but grown successfully at high altitudes. "Take these home to Jo," would be the request. "Tell her, 'thank you!'"

There were almost always thanks in the pain-filled eyes of patients being lifted into the plane to fly to a distant hospital base. Without that evacuation flight there would be nothing ahead but more pain, and probably death. It might only be those eyes that expressed appreciation with a glance or a look. At other times, 'thank you' was expressed almost inaudibly through lips clenched in deep agony and spoken in a language we could not understand.

Such gratitude made our job all the more fulfilling.

THANKS!
Of all the 'thank yous' I have ever received for a flight, one stands out above all others. It wasn't tea on the tailplane. It wasn't fruit or flowers.

For Laurie Darrington and me this flight was unique. In fact, we risked the suspension of our flying licences by doing it.

We flew a small boy back to his island home, more than a hundred and twenty miles off the north coast of Papua New Guinea. We took him home. To die.

This desperately ill child, about twelve years of age, had been brought into the Wewak District Hospital by a Russian oceanographic survey ship. The Russians had found him on an island called Ninigo, and they had brought him to Wewak where they knew there was a good hospital. But nothing could be done for him. He had advanced leukaemia. There was no treatment.

"Couldn't you possibly fly him home?" Risto Gobius, the district medical officer and hospital superintendent, kept asking. "There won't be a boat going out there for months. It would have been better if he had not been brought here. He cries all day and half the night. There's no one here who can speak his language. We can't explain to him that he's going to die. It's so sad. He needs to be with people he knows and loves. You've got a seaplane. Can't you help?"

But we couldn't get approval to do a flight like that. No one had ever flown an aircraft to Ninigo Island. There was little contact with Ninigo other than through a small trading boat that collected the annual copra harvest.

My good friend Risto was very persuasive. "Max, please. Just come out to the hospital and see this kid," he pleaded.

"It can't be done, Risto," I said. But he was insistent.

I finally went. And when I saw the little boy, I knew immediately that it should be done. It had to be done. Risto, Laurie and I would take him.

The day was particularly beautiful. The sea was a deep blue, and wispy clouds flecked the tranquil sky. Beside us on the floor lay our frail little patient. His wasted body was covered in bruise-like lesions, and there were traces of blood around his mouth. Our hearts ached for him.

A vast expanse of ocean had to be crossed. This certainly was not a normal operation. We were looking for an island that none of us had ever seen and where no plane had ever been before.

What an exquisite little place Ninigo turned out to be. A flat, palm-covered green island, it was outlined on one side with clean white sand, on the other with a white line where the gentle breaking surf washed over a coral reef. The water was crystal clear. A resort developer would have been ecstatic! Imagine the potential of this glorious, unspoiled paradise.

There was no smooth water lagoon that we could see. As we circled, we must have attracted the astonished attention of every villager on Ninigo. An aeroplane? Over our island?

It was unheard-of. They were beside themselves with excitement – waving, shouting, jumping. We flew around, trying to find a safe length of quiet water shorewards of the encircling reef. But there was none. Eventually, having noticed the sea was quite calm, I decided to land outside the reef and taxi the aircraft over it, to the beach. We had noticed that the village was near the shoreline.

A group of huge men appeared, running towards the beach from among the nearby coconut trees. They splashed their way through the water to meet us. I cut the engine quickly and steered the aircraft to the shallows. As the first of the men reached us they began to clamber up on to the float. We had to gesture and yell to them to keep clear. A dozen heavy men on one float of a seaplane is a recipe for disaster.

Their obvious leader shouted orders and instructions to the others. We motioned for him, on his own, to climb up on to the pontoon. Then we opened the plane's door.

When he saw the child on the floor, he gasped and uttered a low moan. Instantly, his joy turned to sadness. He turned back and spoke to his men, who were excitedly waiting their turn to see into this strange machine. They were immediately silent. Turning back to the dying boy, he gently and compassionately stroked his face and hair, murmuring soft, comforting words.

For the first time in weeks, the little fellow smiled. He was home.

Two of the men ran off and returned, minutes later, with a large woven mat. They draped it over the aircraft float, and we gently lowered the boy on to it. What followed was a strange and moving ritual.

In absolute silence, like pall-bearers, they carried him high above the crystal clear, warm blue water, to the shore. Then, with soft and harmonious wailing, they moved in solemn procession, off through the trees. We could still hear them long after they were out of sight. These were a deeply grieving people.

We waded around in the shallow waters for a few minutes, not sure what to do next. It didn't seem right for us to intrude. What we had set out to do, out of mercy for a dying boy, had been done. We felt satisfied. But it was strangely anticlimactic for the three of us, standing there alone by the shore.

"Well, we may as well go home," one of us said rather flatly.

But as we were turning the aircraft around and preparing to climb back into it, the village chief appeared again through the trees. With him were a few others. They walked at a solemn pace along the beach, as if on a ceremonial parade. They weren't running, as they had been when we arrived. There were no yells of excitement as they waded to where we were standing by our gently bobbing seaplane.

One by one, they encircled us until we were completely surrounded. Each one of them gently touched us, on our arms and shoulders. It was as if, through physical contact, they felt we could be joined in spirit.

Then the chief, a huge brown man, looked directly at us and with great emotion in his deep resonant voice. *"Mipela tok tenkyu."* ("We say thank you.")

That was all. But it was enough. They waited in silence for a few extra moments. Then these dignified island men turned away again and made their way back to the village, no doubt to join in the grieving and sorrow. I felt like crying. What a 'thank you' that was. What a gift.

I doubt that I will ever go back to Ninigo or see its pristine beauty again. But I am left with an image of an exquisite little tropical island and, somewhere, a small grave in the sand.

BUT NO THANKS!
My little Cessna was exposed, vulnerable, and totally out of place. Another towering grey-green wave, capped with white,

bore down upon it. As the aircraft's nose rose to climb the face of this massive volume of water, the propeller bit into the swirling white cap with a crunching sound and drove high-speed missiles of salt water all over the windscreen and wings.

In the troughs between the unending succession of swells, there appeared to be nothing but ocean surrounding me. But from the crest of each wave, I could make out the lines of coconut palms on the distant shore.

What in the world was I doing here? In this little seaplane? On an angry ocean?

Close to midnight on the previous evening, a group of men had come to our house saying that a small boat was missing along the coast to the west of Wewak. Two men from their fishing club had not returned, they told us. There was a chalkboard by the boat ramp, and every group going beyond the confines of the Wewak bay was required to record where they were intending to fish and the time they planned to return. People seldom stayed out after their nominated return time.

These two men had gone out early in the day, intending to fish along the coast to the west, within twenty miles of the town. They had written on the board that they expected to be back at 6:00pm. But by 9:00pm, when they hadn't arrived, it was obvious that something was wrong.

"We'll wait all night for them," the men said to us. "But if they haven't turned up by daylight, could you please search the area for us and try to find out where they are? Perhaps you could get the plane ready so that you could be in the air right at first light? We feel it's very serious. These guys never stay out late," they said.

The missing boat didn't return during the night.

Next morning, just before dawn, several of us drove to the Wewak market, at the leeward beach of the town, where we kept our float plane. Normally at this time of day there was a bustle of activity. Local village women would be gathering with their bags of smoked fish and flying fox, bananas and mangoes, pineapples and pawpaws, beetle nut, coconuts, and limes, laying them out on woven mats for the day's trading. But it was Sunday and the market was deserted. I parked the MAF van.

The yellow and black seaplane presented an incongruous sight, tied to a trailer on the sand beside the empty market stalls. It had become something of an attraction, but it was safe and secure, nonetheless. In those days, at least.

As the sun began to lighten the eastern sky, we pushed the trailer into the water and floated the seaplane free. I climbed aboard, completed my pre-take-off checks, started the engine, and taxied very carefully through the calm, shallow water barely covering the nearby coral reef, and into the deeper part of the bay. I had removed all the seats from the aircraft to keep it as light as possible, in case I had to land in the open sea.

As I took off I noticed that, unlike the smoother water in the lee of the Wewak headland, the outer ocean was running a heavy swell. A thorough scattering of white caps suggested it was not a day to be out in a fourteen-foot aluminium dinghy. Nor was it a day to land a small float plane, designed for calm waters, in the open sea. Many times we had operated that Cessna in conditions for which I'm sure it was never designed. I had put it down in narrow, swiftly running rivers and even on the ocean. But never in a sea like this.

I flew the prescribed area at two thousand feet about five miles from the coast. There was no sign of a small boat anywhere. With the coast still in sight, I decided to fly on a little farther before heading back and beginning a more 'patterned' search.

At the end of that extra leg I saw the boat. It was miles beyond where I had been told it should be, and in spite of the patches of white on the ocean, it was surprisingly visible in the morning sun. I descended and flew towards it.

The boat was upright but full of water, wallowing in the heavy sea. Only the back was not submerged. Sitting there, on the stern plank, was a man. His head was drooping on his chest and with every roll of the boat it flopped and he would tip, almost falling back into the water. He neither looked up nor waved, even though I flew close by, barely ten feet above the waves. There was no outboard motor. It appeared that at some stage during the night the boat had capsized and the motor with everything else on board had gone to the bottom of the ocean.

It was on my second pass that I noticed the body of the other man, rolling and bobbing in the front of the water-filled boat. My heart sank.

The survivor, wearing no life jacket, was obviously close to the end of his endurance. Clearly, there was little chance for him. Unless something drastic was done. A rescue boat would take hours to get to this position from Wewak.

I was utterly perplexed. Even to attempt a landing in these mountainous seas would be madness. But could it be done? I looked hard at the lines of swells and wondered, if indeed I did manage to pull off a landing, how I would ever get airborne again. And how could I get that fellow on board anyway? I was on my own! I would have to climb down out of the cockpit to help him. Who would control the aircraft? I prayed desperately.

This man's life was in my hands.

I tried to judge the height of the waves. I looked at the waterlogged boat to see how it rose and fell. I even counted the frequency of the breaking swells. White caps looked pretty from higher up. Now they were angry and ominous.

Nonetheless, I was fairly sure I could get down. And I felt I had a better than even chance of at least getting the man out of the boat and on board. But I was far from sure that I could take off again. *Perhaps*, I thought, *I can land, pick him up, and then just taxi to the lee of the small island I had noticed a few miles away.* But even taxiing in such conditions would be extremely demanding, if not impossible. The wind was blowing right across the swells. Any take-off would have to be made crosswind along the swells. In a sea as heavy as this, it would be an extremely risky procedure.

I was also worried about the aircraft's propeller. I had seen before the effect upon a propeller when impacted by salt water at high speed. The leading edge of the blade rapidly splits, almost folding it open.

But how could I just fly back to Wewak, leaving this man alone in a disabled boat, to die? With a pounding heart, I determined to try to rescue him.

I reduced power, configured the aircraft for landing, and set up my approach. I had to land crosswind, along the heaving swell lines. At the first smack of dark-green ocean water, I jerked the throttle closed and pulled back hard on the control column. The plane stopped quickly.

Almost immediately, the aircraft tilted forty-five degrees as it rode sideways up one swell, and perched for a split second high on the water. I could see the coast. But then, with the same degree of 'bank', this time to the port, I slid down the other face of the wave.

It was very difficult to taxi. In spite of pressure to the rudders, the waves and wind tugged at the aircraft, seeking to 'weathercock' it into the wind. I was also aware that colliding with the edges of the metal boat would quickly puncture the floats. Finally, I managed to position myself as close as I dared alongside the waterlogged dinghy. It was too heavy to ride over the top of the swells, and every broken white cap threatened to wash the fisherman from his perch in the stern.

Suddenly, with a start, he became conscious of my presence. An aircraft? Out here on the water? It must have been beyond his belief. He immediately tried to stand up and reach towards me.

"Sit down!" I yelled through the open window, against the noise of the engine. "Don't try to get up. I'll come alongside. Don't do anything until you hear my engine stop. Then jump for the plane. I'll get you."

He understood. His ashen face bore a mixed expression of fear, hope and desperation.

As I approached the boat on the third try, I cut the engine, opened the door, and jumped out on to the float. It was wet and slick. I felt exposed and vulnerable as the wind buffeted me and the spray whipped at my face. *What will happen if I fall into the water?* I thought. Now uncontrolled, the plane immediately began to turn into the wind, pointing its nose at the oncoming swells. "Now, jump!" I screamed. He did so, and I grabbed his jacket at the neck and pulled him across the float. He lay there for a moment while I clung to the strut. Then, with great difficulty, I manhandled his sodden body on board and scrambled in after him.

Safe! Well, at least, away from the water.

Climbing quickly into my seat I turned the ignition key. "Please, God, let it start," I prayed. The engine roared into life again. The whirling propeller spat water across the windscreen. *Whatever are those propeller blades like?* I worried, as I turned to taxi once more along the swells. I hadn't even thought to check. I prayed that they were not too damaged. There was nothing I could do about it anyway.

My passenger by this time was sitting at the back of the cabin on the floor with his head up against the rear bulkhead.

I taxied by the boat once more. I felt awful leaving that body, rolling around in the water, caught in the boat's superstructure. But any more effort to recover it would have been foolish in the extreme. Feeling heavy-hearted, I turned the aircraft away.

There were still grave doubts that we could get airborne again. An island five miles to the east was probably within reach, but I could see now that taxiing there was impossible. Fortunately I had used a good quantity of fuel and the aircraft, lighter now, was sitting higher in the water. I advised Wewak that I was getting airborne again, and once more lined the plane up along the swells.

At first, even with full power, it didn't seem as if we were going to move. With each massive wave, one wing would drop as we climbed the lee side, and then in a lazy roll, the other would fall away as we slipped down the face.

Sheets of water poured over the engine and wings as the plane began to move. The air-speed indicator wasn't registering anything at all. The Pitot head – the external air-speed sensor – was full of sea water.

With the engine screaming, and undoubtedly with spray flying in a gigantic plume behind us, the seaplane began to pick up speed. Between wave tops we would accelerate further, only to have the momentum decrease as we ploughed through a crest. I could only hope and pray that eventually, we might become airborne.

Suddenly, we were suspended, barely in the air as we leapt from the top of a huge swell. Perhaps it was not so much that the plane got airborne but rather that the water underneath just dropped away! With my right hand I grabbed a couple of 'notches' of flap. I thought we were going to hit again at the bottom of the next trough. But we didn't, and the aircraft clawed its way over the oncoming wall of water.

The air-speed indicator still read zero. The system was indeed blocked with sea water. But we really were flying! I reported my departure to Wewak and gave them an estimate for arrival at the town beach.

"Request report on the state of the survivors," was their quick response.

"Wewak, there is only one survivor," I replied. They did not ask for a name or for more information.

Back on the smooth water of the bay, I taxied towards the small crowd waiting on the beach behind the market place. I was so grateful to God and thankful to be safely back.

Two women stood thigh-deep in the water. Both were waiting for their husbands. It was heart-wrenching. The memory of a partly submerged, bluish body out there in the ocean haunted me. Who was he? What was he like? Which of these two women was his wife?

Jo drove me home from the beach that Sunday. I was exhausted. It was so good to be back. The plane needed a thorough wash down and a new propeller. Otherwise it was fine. The Cessna. What a marvellous aircraft.

All that afternoon I wondered what was happening in the town. How were they going to recover the body? How was the man I had rescued? It would be good to talk with him. On the flight back to Wewak he had told me that they had caught a lot of fish during the afternoon; there were large bags of them in the centre of the boat. But broadside to a huge freak wave, the bags of fish had suddenly slipped right across the floor and the craft had capsized. The motor was torn from its mounting and immediately sank. The restraining chain had snapped.

Unfortunately, the bucket in which they had placed all the required emergency gear was not secured, and also disappeared into the rising sea. Then darkness fell.

His friend had died during the night and the survivor, so traumatised by the shocking experience, had become quite hallucinatory. He told me that hundreds of sea snakes had come into the boat as it filled with water and had killed his friend. I did hear later, however, that it was revealed that his mate had died from a heart attack.

During the next few days I fully expected someone to come, at least to talk to me about the events of that morning. Perhaps, even, to say thank you.

But no one ever came.

Maybe the survivor had left town quickly. No doubt the awful shock and trauma of the experience would have had a devastating effect on him. I never heard from him again. Not a word.

And as the years have gone by, the memory of it has always seemed, somehow, unfinished.

These are stories about one life that was saved and two that were lost. But they are really stories about giving thanks. They illustrate a basic human need. To be affirmed. To be appreciated. To be thanked. Even Jesus felt hurt when only one leper came back to thank Him for the healing he had received. "Where are the other nine?" Jesus asked.

The psalmist knew a lot about saying thank you. Over and over he calls us to give thanks to God for all that He has done. "Enter his gates with thanksgiving and his courts with praise; give thanks to him and praise his name." (Psalm 100:4)

It is the same in the New Testament. "Be joyful always; pray continually; give thanks in all circumstances, for this is God's will for you in Christ Jesus." (1 Thessalonians 5:16–18)

The people at Ninigo, even in their grief, came back to say, *"Tenkyu"*. And we felt wonderfully rewarded.

Have you thanked anyone lately?

Have you thanked God lately?

PART 3

21

Destination Down Under

I will never leave you nor forsake you.

Joshua 1:5

The Spirit of God was hovering over the waters.

Genesis 1:2

We all have our heroes.

When I was growing up, every Australian boy knew the name Charles Kingsford Smith. He was one of my heroes. In 1928 he made history by becoming the first man to fly across the Pacific Ocean. And he was Australian. Of course!

The story of that flight makes fascinating reading.

For more than seven thousand miles, at the breakneck speed of ninety miles per hour, he lumbered over the vast expanse of the Pacific Ocean in an old Fokker tri-motor aircraft, romantically named *The Southern Cross*.

'Smithy', as he was popularly known, had an Aussie co-pilot, Charles Ulm, and an American navigator, Harry Lyon, who until that flight had only navigated ships across the ocean! Their radio operator was another American, Jim Warner.

Just picturing that ancient aeroplane, crawling its way

through the lonely Pacific skies and over endless ocean, is mind-boggling to me. I can hardly imagine it. Twenty-seven hours from Oakland to Honolulu, and thirty-four more to Suva, in Fiji. At Suva there wasn't even an airstrip. They landed on a downtown sports ground and, after refuelling, the aircraft was towed to a nearby beach for take-off. The flight from Fiji to Australia, hours of it spent in almost uncontrollable turbulence in line after line of electrical storms, was a short twenty-two hours!

Intrepid is a word that was often used in those days of the feats of amazing men, though one could say that 'Smithy' and his crew were *mad.*

As for me – I dreamed of the day when I too would do it! Fly an aeroplane right across the Pacific Ocean!

Of course, by that time transoceanic flight was almost routine. As children, our dad would take us to Sydney's 'Kingsford Smith' Airport to watch the planes. Some of them would make the journey daily. But these were DC-6s, Stratoclippers and Constellations – giant aircraft with inspiring names. Certainly not 'rag-and-wire' creations like Smithy's old Fokker.

So when my chance came, there wasn't a moment's hesitation. Would I do it? Oh yes!

My 'epic' flight, in 1973, was from MAF's US base at Fullerton Municipal Airport in Orange Country, Los Angeles, to Melbourne, Australia. My aircraft was to be a twin-engined Piper Aztec. Nothing fancy. And certainly not a Fokker trimotor. But enough to call for an adventurous spirit.

This was the opportunity of a lifetime!

MAF in Australia had purchased the aircraft from a board member of MAF in the USA. The plane was needed for mission and church work in the eastern province of Indonesia. It was to be based at Kupang, in Timor. A single-engined Cessna had been used in the initial stage of the programme's development, but with so much overwater flying, a light twin would be more appropriate.

In preparation for the long flight, the four passenger seats had been removed and replaced with an enormous rubber fuel tank. This was built into a wooden frame on the cabin floor. All the connections to take the extra gas had been professionally installed and checked. We had a flight endurance of something in excess of twenty-three hours, more than enough for our longest leg.

One of MAF's senior American pilots, Hank Worthington, had agreed to make the flight with me. I don't think Hank had to be talked into it either.

We flew the aircraft from Los Angeles to Oakland, California, our departure point for the first leg. This gave us the shortest track to Hawaii. On the day before the flight, not having been to San Francisco before, I took a fascinating bus tour of the city and surrounding area. As we passed by a certain part of the bay, our driver and tour guide, chattering informatively, said, "Ladies and gentlemen, this part of the bay is where the giant 'clipper' flying boats used to take off on their long journey to Honolulu. They would struggle off the water and climb ever so slowly out to the ocean. Would you believe it?" he said, "A thirteen-hour flight!" Gasps of disbelief were heard from all over the bus.

I smiled pensively and stared at the thin blue horizon. We had just completed our flight plan. The first leg? Fifteen-and-a-half hours.

The Aztec is a very docile aircraft. A good performer, it climbs well, and under normal conditions has reliable single-engined performance. In our case, an extra fuel load of more than a thousand pounds put us way beyond maximum gross weight. When I was flying jet fighters, we used to make scathing comments about aircraft with less performance than ours. "Flies like a ruptured duck," we'd snort. Hank and I were about to see just how ruptured our little duck was going to be.

"Taxi to the threshold of the short runway," the air traffic controller said, as we requested clearance. Hank's response was crisp. "Er, we'll take the long one, thanks." We were given clearance and lined up, grossly overloaded. This was to be the longest flight I had ever made.

Take-off was surprisingly normal, and I was astonished at how quickly the aircraft became airborne. But while the plane had no problems getting off the ground, its climb perform-ance was an entirely different matter. Foot by painstaking foot, our flying fuel tank clawed its way upwards. It took a full hour to reach our chosen cruising altitude of ten thousand five hundred feet. I had read that when Kingsford Smith departed Oakland for Hawaii, with their fuel load of four tons, they took even longer than that to reach their cruising altitude – of fifteen hundred feet! As we entered San Francisco Bay and headed out across the mighty Pacific, I thought again of those magnificent men in their flying machines. Fifteen hundred feet was barely enough altitude to escape the ocean salt spray. Amazing courage.

"Have a safe flight," said the traffic controller as he passed us over to the area flight-service frequency.

Time crawled by – one slow hour after another. The sun was still high in the sky. Our ETA at Honolulu was 2:30am local time! We had a long way to go.

"Just follow the contrails," the experts had said about finding one's way from San Francisco to Honolulu. "There is such a density of traffic on that route." But we saw no condensation trails. The sky was a clear, uncluttered blue. It was a magnificent day. The ocean below, however, looked more intimidating. It was littered with white caps. We didn't have much information about the wind at our altitude, and for all we knew it could have been blowing us miles off track.

In these modern days of satellite-reading, global positioning systems, a ferry pilot can know his exact location at any time – to within about seventy-five feet. For us it was mostly guesswork. We didn't even have good communication with the ground, and, as expected, it was not long before our one automatic direction finder (radio compass) was out of range of the coastal beacons. The needle on the instrument first began to waver and then to turn – slowly, around and around – for hour after hour.

There was a respite of sorts halfway into that fifteen-hour mix of boredom and concern. In the early seventies, a ship was stationed midway between the west coast of the USA and Honolulu to assist in aircraft navigation. Its radio call sign was 'Ocean Station November', and great was our delight when we made contact with the radio operators who spent their time way out there in the ocean. It was reassuring to hear a human voice. It was even more reassuring to find that we were right on track and on time.

Our major concern was oil usage in the engines. Flights in an Aztec would usually average only two or three hours, thus there was no need for an oil contents gauge in the cabin. But our fifteen-hour flight over the open ocean was somewhat different. Oil usage was indeed a worry.

So we just sat and waited. On and on. Strapped in. No getting up to stretch. No walking around. And all we saw was that ocean. 'Flying the Pond' is the term used for such ferry flights. Some pond! And this first fifteen-hour section was only a third of the total distance across it.

What a relief when, about thirteen hours after take-off, the radio compass needle began to respond to a beacon far ahead. It had been going round and around slowly for hours. First, almost imperceptibly, it hesitated in the 'dead-ahead' position. It was beginning to recognise the Honolulu beacon. By this time it was long since dark. We could no longer see the white caps below. The needle finally stopped. It had found the beacon. The airport, the white beach of Waikiki, coconut palms – and a bed – were out there in the darkness, waiting for us. We were nearly there.

There had been no voice contact on the radio for many hours, just the constant crackle of static. Then suddenly we heard, "Aztec Six Six Three Six Yankee, this is Honolulu Centre, do you read?" What a welcome voice!

Another living soul was out there.

The flickering lights of Honolulu were a kaleidoscope of colour, even at 2:00am. But they didn't shine for us nearly as brightly as did the two lines of white runway lights stretching before us, guiding us down as we made our final approach.

Terra firma! We thanked God for our safe arrival.

Having been directed to the appropriate parking bay, we shut down the engines. I opened the door, took a flashlight, and jumped down on to the ground. Why did my legs feel like jelly and the tarmac strangely insecure? I hurried to undo the cowl flap and measure the oil contents. How much had each engine used? I really wanted to know whether our concern was justified. We didn't want to fly over even more remote stretches of ocean, constantly worried about oil consumption.

But there were almost ten quarts in each engine. We'd hardly used any oil at all. In more than fifteen hours! I sighed with relief.

An hour or so later, both of us fell into bed and were immediately lost in the blissful oblivion of deep sleep.

When we woke, we felt exhilarated. Ready for the next leg.

And so, on to Pago Pago, American Samoa, in the South Pacific.

We took off from Honolulu around noon, with a flight-planned time of sixteen-and-a-half hours! No land mass en route. No islands – not within hundreds of miles. And this time there would be no 'Ocean Station' ship positioned halfway along the route. In fact, very few planes of any kind crossed this particular segment of ocean.

Again, heavily laden with fuel, we fought our way to cruising altitude. The radio compass gave us a reasonable back bearing on Honolulu for about two hours. Then, we knew, for twelve hours we would have nothing until we would be able to receive transmissions from the beacon at Pago Pago. Below, huge rolling swells and monstrous waves, topped with the blowing spume from white caps, stretched behind and endlessly before us.

We droned on for over eight hours, tracking south from Honolulu, cocooned and uncomfortable. We had no accurate idea of our position. We were following a compass heading, but, of course, who was to know what effect the prevailing winds were having? Were we on track? Or perhaps twenty miles off? Or a hundred? There was no way of knowing and nothing we could do. Except wait for another five or six hours, when the next beacon would, hopefully, identify Pago Pago some distance out. We talked a lot but both felt the underlying tension of our situation.

Then somewhat unexpectedly a voice broke the airwaves. An airline pilot was reporting his position en route from Nandi, Fiji, to Honolulu. We couldn't hear the response to his call but figured he was somewhere in our area, probably within a few hundred miles. We were not alone! We could hardly wait for him to finish his report. Then we called him up, identified ourselves, and asked him to call us back on 121.5, the short-range VHF emergency frequency. No one else could hear us using this wavelength.

"Did you say 'Aztec' Six Six Three Six Yankee?" he asked, with a southern American drawl, when we established contact on VHF.

"Affirmative."

"Do you mean a Piper Aztec? A twin-engined Piper Aztec?" His tone of voice betrayed his amazement.

"Affirmative," we again responded.

There was silence. Then, with incredulity, he asked, "Man, what are you doin' way out here? In that little-bitty aircraft?"

"We're going to Australia!" Hank replied with a grin.

And so began an unforgettable radio conversation. Initially, we requested him to tilt his radar to its lowest angle, hoping he might be able to make contact with us. "We'd love to know exactly where we are." We didn't tell him we had no idea of our actual position. But he couldn't see us on his radar screen. We were disappointed.

"Tell me! What are you guys doin'?" he said. And so we told him of our flight from Oakland the previous day. Hank asked him to pass on an 'operations normal' call to Honolulu Centre for us. Then we talked about the great differences in our aircraft, about his four-engined jet, about his height and speed, and ours. We discussed his route, his crew, his passengers, and so on. We laughed a lot. And joked with each other.

"Hey, PanAm! How about sendin' down some of them grain-fed, three-inch Texan steaks y'all are servin' in first class!"

"Why, what are you guys eating?" he inquired.

"We're eating Fritos down here!" Hank responded. He crackled the Fritos packet close to the microphone. "Thirty-three packets and countin'!"

The 707 captain laughed. We must have chatted for thirty to forty minutes as he sped northwards at about five hundred knots, and we, far below, lumbered on southwards at about a hundred and twenty. Finally he said goodbye. That contact with another human voice had been wonderfully therapeutic in our lonely, exposed flight.

About five minutes later, however, we heard that friendly voice again.

"Hey, Aztec! You still there?" Hank smiled at me.

"I've been talkin' to my girls about you." (We assumed he meant the stewardesses on his crew.) "We're a bit concerned. We reckon if we was you, and you was us, we'd like you to keep on talkin' for a while. So let's keep this thing goin'!"

And he went on to tell us about a fishing lodge he had on Victoria Island, off Vancouver, and the Cessna 180 seaplane he 'played with' when he was there. He told us about the families of all his crew, where they came from, what they did for relaxation. Trivia, but much appreciated entertainment.

We in turn told him about MAF and its unique use of aircraft in mission.

Our conversation continued until we began to lose contact with each other because of the widening distance between us. Eventually, the transmissions began to break up, and we signed off.

Once again, the hours went slowly by.

In loneliness, in isolation, the power of a human voice is profound. Hank and I wondered, as we flew along, how many people, probably millions right at that moment, longed to hear a human voice. Not people exposed to the kind of extreme isolation we were experiencing, but people sitting in homes, in apartments, perhaps in some of the busiest places on earth. We had friends, loved ones, who were waiting and praying for us. But who cared for all these others? In that time of absolute isolation, we realised how powerfully effective a human voice can be.

Someone once wrote, "What is life to one for whom no one waits?" What, indeed.

Night came on. A pitch-black, cloudless Pacific night. The stars were crystal clear and quite brilliant. We watched a satellite slowly make its way across the heavens and wondered whether it might be a space capsule. Perhaps someone was up there, like us sitting in cramped isolation, far from home.

It was easy and natural to think about God. The astounding thought, as we droned our way slowly across that mighty ocean under a canopy of those millions of bright, shining stars, was that God knew precisely where we were. He didn't need a puny man-made global positioning system. He knew – exactly – and He did care.

We felt safe.

Eventually, as it had the previous night, the searching needle of the radio compass once more began to indicate that there was a beacon out there ahead of us, hundreds of miles away. Initially again, it hesitated from its monotonous circling, at the 'right on the nose' position, and finally caught the pulse of a signal. After a few more rotations it settled happily to a stop, pointing to our destination out there in the darkness. Pago Pago! Only a little place. But oh, how welcome!

And so we landed there at about 3:00am on a balmy tropical night.

Having eventually found a hotel, we once again flopped on to our beds and were soon peacefully asleep. We didn't realise until about 10:00am that we had been taken to a glitzy tourist resort and the entire wall of our room was glass – right at sand level! Outside was a glorious, wide, sun-drenched tropical beach. The blue sea glistened in the morning sun, fifty yards away. The curtains were totally open, and tanned-skinned, beautiful people traipsed by, curiously looking in at two semi-clad men draped over the beds, sound asleep in the middle of the morning. How fortunate that we had not entirely disrobed in our exhaustion.

The flight to Auckland, New Zealand, later that day was relatively short. Only ten hours. As we flew over Vavah'u, a northern island of the Kingdom of Tonga, we looked down on dozens of yachts moored in the magnificent bay there. Vavah'u is a haven for oceanic 'yachties'. We wondered what they thought of us as we passed overhead.

Rain was bucketing down when we landed at Auckland International Airport to be met by friends from MAF New Zealand. A layover of twenty-four hours and the company of these good people were a welcome interlude. Rain was still falling when we departed the following day for Melbourne. Was this an omen?

The meteorological office in Auckland could not tell us with any accuracy the wind speed at ten thousand feet, our proposed altitude for the last part of our journey. They did know that there were reports of severe weather over the Tasman Sea. "It's a slow-moving system and seems to be stuck out there," they told us. "If you were flying at thirty-five thousand feet, we would have more accurate weather for you, but airline pilots are reporting significant build-ups mid-Tasman. Reports of occasional lightning."

Significant build-ups? Occasional lightning?

By the time we had trundled five hours out across the ocean, Hank and I were in one accord. The New Zealand meteorological officers had been just a tad conservative. By then, 'significant' and 'occasional' had become 'horrendous' and 'unrelenting'. There were brilliant flashes all around us. Without radar, the best we could do was simply head for the area of the sky that seemed to be least affected by towering, violent electrical storms. But there was no avoiding them.

It made no sense to turn around and fly back to Auckland. Huge thunderheads, filled with bursts of intense white light, completely encircled us. We pressed on.

The entire region of the mid-Tasman that night was a mass of turbulent weather. Each time we entered cloud, massive bursts of hissing, roaring electricity flashed around, illuminating the entire sky. Sizzling bolts of power exploded into the boiling sea below. The Aztec itself appeared aglow, like a neon tube. I'd seen this phenomenon before. Saint Elmo's fire. Static electricity painted circles of fire around the tips of the propellers, while snaking worms of electricity raced over the windscreen and around the cabin glass.

Worst of all was the turbulence. Although we had the automatic pilot engaged, it was all we could do simply to hold the aircraft straight and level. We were thrown from side to side, at one moment being pressed down into our seats, the next, weightless! The plane felt like a leaf being blown around in a storm. The experience was at once extremely dangerous and incredibly exhilarating. In the excitement of the thunder, the sizzling streaks of lightning, and the impossibly violent turbulence, we lost all thought of the risk. It was the ride of a lifetime!

We couldn't read the compass, but it didn't matter. Whether we were forced to divert to the right or left of track was somewhat immaterial. After all, we were not likely to miss Australia! So for more than two hours we just hung on and fought to keep the plane in the air.

At one point, I recall thinking, *Mr Piper, you made a sturdy aircraft when you made this Aztec*. It just kept ploughing on through the storms, hail and horrendous buffeting. Not once did we detect even the slightest sound of discord in the note of those two engines. They just sang on, in harmony, almost as if they were as determined to complete the journey as the two men struggling at the controls.

Then, suddenly, after about two or three hours, we burst out of the western side of that band of awe-inspiring storms into calm, smooth air.

Soon the coastline of eastern Victoria came into view. Long stretches of yellow sand and the endless lines of crashing white breakers marked the 'Ninety Mile' beach. Inland, Victoria's eastern lakes and heavily timbered mountains painted a tranquil and beautiful scene.

Home! Australia!

The landing at Essendon Airport was uneventful, almost an anticlimax. Jo was there with a few MAF friends to meet us. We soon had the aircraft cleared by the customs officials, and I was on the way home – for a good long rest. My five boys were fascinated with the tale I had to tell.

I'd done it! At last. But never again!

I never looked for the opportunity to do it again.

'Smithy', in *The Southern Cross*, spent eighty-three hours in the air on his remarkable journey. It took us just fifty-five!

With hardly an hour or two to catch his breath, my friend Hank went out to the International Airport at Melbourne and caught a plane back to the USA! Hank was tougher than I.

I have often reflected on that crossing. It was a wonderful, unforgettable experience. I had always dreamed of making such a flight. We flew a considerable distance around the world in a tiny little plane. Just a brave little dot, winging its way over the sea.

And as I've looked back upon it, I have thought about how small and insignificant we were, squeezed into a tiny cabin, unable to get out of our seats or even to get up to stretch. So vulnerable. Had there been a mechanical failure out there somewhere, someone might have found us. But it would have been unlikely.

Did anyone know precisely where we were?

God knew.

He tells us that He knows even when a sparrow falls to the ground.

People are more valuable than sparrows. And God knows each and every one. Wherever we are, and in whatever predicament. When we long to hear another human voice, when loneliness eats its way to the depth of our being and we are buffeted and losing control, surely one of life's greatest treasures is to hear an inner voice guiding us home, reminding us.

22

Light Over Darkness

"I am the light of the world. Whoever follows me will never walk in darkness, but will have the light of life."

John 8:12

"You are the light of the world . . . let your light shine before men, that they may see your good deeds and praise your Father in heaven."

Matthew 5:14,16

In April 1994, Jo and I made a flight from Los Angeles to Johannesburg, South Africa, right at the time the conflict in Rwanda was about to explode. Newspapers and TV reports were full of stories of a terrible human disaster taking place in that beautiful country. Killing sprees were predicted to escalate even further, and there was talk of total genocide. It seemed that the larger nations were doing little to stop this tragedy. A friend told me the previous week that he had seen a mass of corpses bouncing in the foaming water at the base of a waterfall on the Rwanda-Tanzania border.

The agony at Rwanda during that time is now history. It seems beyond belief that eight hundred thousand people could have died there in just a hundred days of mad rampage.

At London's Heathrow Airport, Jo and I tried to keep abreast of the news in Rwanda. We had arrived there, already weary, at 6:00am. Now, we were facing a fourteen-hour layover before the flight to Africa. What news we could get was very disturbing.

An evacuation on a massive scale was taking place. A large proportion of the Rwandan population, mainly Hutu people, was seeking safety in neighbouring Zaire. More than a million had already crossed the border at Goma and Bukavu. More were expected. The increasing danger was that there would be an outbreak of disease among the refugees in the appalling and totally insanitary conditions. It was a dark time in African history, a political and tribal conflict that few people outside Rwanda could ever hope to understand.

The TV monitors in the airport showed video confirming our worst fears. Not only was Goma and the surrounding countryside occupied by up to one and a half million Rwandan refugees, but cholera had broken out there. Disenfranchised, hungry, traumatised people, many of whom had witnessed unbelievable horror in recent days, were dying by the thousands.

While still at Heathrow I confirmed my plans to fly on to Goma from Johannesburg. We had a conference to attend, but it was more important that I visit MAF staff in eastern Zaire. A time of intense pressure, I needed to ascertain what part MAF could play in the huge relief effort that would be necessary. I also just wanted to 'be there' with our Zaire staff. Superb people.

We had been 'on the road' twenty-eight hours already and had at least another twelve to go before we touched down at Jan Smuts Airport in South Africa. Finally we boarded, and after a further two-hour technical delay, the aircraft was pushed back from the gate. Great, now we might get a few hours' sleep.

The captain, having first apologised for the delay, said, "I'm afraid that we are expecting some rather bumpy weather during the first few hours of our long flight tonight. Other flights have experienced severe turbulence. After we cross into North Africa, though, it should settle down and be calm for the rest of the flight." Just what we needed!

For those first two hours the aircraft seemed to chase the thunderstorms! Lightning cracked all around us. The cabin crew remained tightly strapped into their seats along with the white-knuckled passengers. As we bounced around like a cork in the surf, I noticed a phenomenon that I had seldom seen since my Air Force days. 'Saint Elmo's fire' dashed across the outside of the windows and along the skin of the aircraft.

There were sighs of relief when the weather finally calmed down and all on board tried to rest for the remaining nine or ten hours of the flight.

Very few of the exhausted passengers bothered to watch the in-flight movie. Most tried to grab a few hours of sleep. Wide awake, I eased out of my seat and made my way down to the back of the plane. After standing there for a while, I lowered the small collapsible cabin-crew seat fixed to the rear bulkhead and strapped myself in. I had the small, square rear-door window all to myself. But there was nothing to be seen in the darkness of the night outside apart from the regular flash of the aircraft's wing-tip navigation light.

Hours must have gone by when, suddenly, something caught my attention in the sky, breaking the intense darkness outside. Faraway, hundreds of miles to the east, small flashes of lightning like tiny, white fireworks burst in the night. I knew, however, that at the actual location of the storm, which probably sat over the centre or the east of Zaire, they would not be tiny flashes. These were crashing, brilliant, thundering bursts of power, probably generated by as violent a weather system as the one that had made this huge aircraft seem so vulnerable just a few hours ago over the Mediterranean. But from my small square window I could only see the black darkness with intermittent flashes, minute specks of white light out there, somewhere. It was fascinating.

This storm could well have been pouring its fury upon the million and a half refugee Rwandans huddled together on the bare, black lava rock around Goma. There would be no shelter for them.

And from my unique vantage point at forty thousand feet, I prayed for them.

I watched the eastern sky begin to lighten.

The night had been long, but the sun was coming.

In the awakening dawn, the intermittent spots of white lightning flashes disappeared. I'm sure the storm didn't cease. It was just that the light that was coming was more intense, brighter than that faraway lightning. The greater new light simply chased the smaller light away!

It was a spectacular dawn. A wonderful kaleidoscope of colour seemed to reach up over the darkness that covered the mass of the African continent, and then descend upon it. As it had chased away the random flashes of the faraway lightning, so it now chased away the darkness across that entire land mass. Night gave way to day, a clear, bright, shining day, revealing the wonderful vista of beautiful Africa. Great rivers, majestic mountains, vast plains, and lush jungles.

Everything that I could now see had been there all the time, but it had been enshrouded in darkness.

Jesus' words, "I am the light of the world," filled my mind.

Just as the sun that morning chased away the darkness of a long night, revealing a panorama of great beauty, I knew that even the horrendous and agonising darkness of Rwanda could be driven away by the light of God's love. I prayed again for the people of Rwanda. I prayed that the greater light – that 'eternal light' – would shine into their darkness.

As I sat there, alone alongside 'my' window that morning, I felt a special closeness to the One who is the 'light of the world'. I offered to Him my deep thanks that His plans had included me. I thanked Him for deeming me worthy of a place in the light.

But this unique 'devotion at dawn' was not over. Some other Scriptures came to mind. Interesting words that the Apostle John recorded Jesus as having said. "While I am in the world I am the light of the world."

While I am in the world? I thought. *What did that mean?*

Then in Matthew's record, another of the sayings of Jesus.

"You are the light of the world."

Twelve men, and ordinary men at that – the light of the world?

I pondered the two similar yet very different statements. It seemed almost blasphemous to take upon ourselves something that was true of the Lord Jesus. But it was Jesus who said it. I reconciled for myself this seeming contradiction. Because those who are committed to Him become channels through which the eternal and divine light of the world shines, He infuses His life into those who follow Him. In truth, they do become the light of the world.

Divine delegation, divine empowerment. But what responsibility!

Two days later I stood on the black lava rock of Goma, Zaire. Hundreds of thousands of Rwandan refugees stood or sat, shoulder to shoulder, as far as I could see. There was no shelter for them other than small, blue plastic tarpaulins, distributed by United Nations workers. There was overwhelming suffering, total bewilderment and agony of soul.

One particular little boy stood out. Before crossing the border from Rwanda, he had seen both his parents hacked to pieces with a machete in front of his eyes. When he arrived, the relief workers told me, he was talking. But he ceased talking the next day, and they couldn't get him to say another word. For four days now, he had been standing in the open air at the relief centre, staring vacantly into space. He was living a horrible nightmare.

By the time I arrived, the relief effort was already in full swing. Military aircraft from all the major nations were landing one after the other to disgorge hundreds of tons of food and clothing. High in the sky, tanker aircraft were refuelling the US and other military aircraft as they headed back to Europe and America to reload. Men in camouflage fatigues were everywhere. Helicopters whipped dust into clouds as they took off to distribute food.

I watched American and French military bulldozers cover a huge hole, the mass grave where thousands of unidentified Rwandan cholera victims had been buried. The drivers wore masks over their faces. It didn't smell nice there.

Amidst this overwhelming horror and tragedy, my thoughts returned to 'my' sunrise.

And to the light of the world.

A beautiful young lady, standing out in a predominantly male crowd at the airport, told me that she had come from Manchester, England, to help out. "I'm a trauma nurse," she said, "and I simply couldn't stand to see the footage of this tragedy on the television without responding. I resigned my job yesterday and flew down here on the evening plane. I've come to do what I can for as long as it takes. This awful tragedy of human life must break God's heart."

The light of the world. It was there – in her! She had come, bringing the light with her.

A team of African doctors and nurses who had flown thousands of miles from their mission hospital in West Africa were achieving small miracles, saving lives in a hastily erected tent clinic. They too had brought the light of the world. It shone through them as it did through so many others driven there by a godly compassion.

When we had landed at Goma the previous day, we had taxied our small MAF Cessna between huge military transport planes from many countries that were disgorging tons of food and relief supplies. An American missionary who had been in that area for fifty years met us. Tears streamed down his face. "I'm so glad you've come," he said. My reply was probably rather flippant. I thought the meagre few hundred pounds of supplies in our plane were less than insignificant. "Yes, but the difference is that you are here to care for the spirits of the people."

You see, MAF also carries the light of the world.

Jesus, the light of the world, stands central in history as in eternity, to drive away darkness.

And it is He who said, "You are the light of the world."

23

Timbuktu

I, even I, am the LORD, and apart from me there is no saviour.

Isaiah 43:11

Timbuktu. What a name!

When I was a boy, Timbuktu was an imaginary place, a fantasy, created by writers of adventure stories for boys. A favourite 'rainy day' book of my childhood described the sandy streets, the ancient mudbrick dwellings, and the shimmering heat of its desert horizons.

So when, in 1987, I found myself wandering those same sandy streets with Jo, I smiled, recalling much-loved tales and legends of faraway places. For this was no work of fiction, no fanciful excursion of the imagination. This was real. We were actually there, in Timbuktu. Fascinating and exotic still, Timbuktu in reality conjured up images of an adventure. Even for grown-up boys.

Timbuktu is an ancient place, steeped in the mystical charm of an ancient desert culture. To its twenty-five thousand inhabitants, it is home. Muslim pilgrims from all over Africa visit the magnificent centuries-old mosque that stands there with heavy wooden beams protruding through the mudbrick outside walls. A revered place, a holy shrine in the world of Islam.

For century upon century, camel travellers and passers-by have stopped there to rest and gather supplies. To them, Timbuktu stands as a welcome respite from the slow, laborious plod across the wastelands of the Sahara.

It is also a place of rich heritage and history. In the twelfth century, one of the world's most prestigious universities was established there. The nearby Niger River also made this a verdant place, a place of luxuriant growth, of trade and wealth. Then, the sands of the Sahara were still a distance to the north.

Over the centuries, however, the sand has moved inexorably closer with each passing year. From the north the Sahara has made its advance, inching its way south, slowly robbing Timbuktu of the richness, the greenery, the fertility. Today it stands remote, magnificent. A city engulfed in sand. Yet it remains still a place of great pride for the people of the Republic of Mali.

Nouh Ag Infa Yatara, 'Pastor Nouh', one of the finest young men I have ever met, was our guide that day. A dark-skinned man of great dignity and presence. Nouh is a shepherd. A shepherd of believers. In a city of twenty-five thousand, Nouh is the pastor of just twenty people who name the Name of Jesus.

Nouh's story of coming to faith in Christ is almost beyond belief.

As a small boy he was caught stealing vegetables. The owner of the garden, a white man, a missionary, gave him the vegetables to keep. But he also gave him some cards upon which were written Bible verses. "If you learn those verses," he said, "I will give you a pen." A great prize for a young man at Timbuktu. But with the learning of those precious words of Scripture came not just a pen, but also the dawning light of conviction that these newly acquired words were true. As he learnt more, the light of God shone into his soul.

But the words Nouh so eagerly continued to learn and his new-found faith brought shame and humiliation to the family. Their son had defiled their home. His talk of the Christian Gospel put his very life in danger. And the threat became a dreadful reality when, because of the stand he took for Jesus, he was given a meal laced with deadly poison. He ate the food, but the wonder of his testimony is that it did him no harm. It paralysed his brother with whom he shared it!

Determination and total commitment to live for Jesus have permeated Nouh's life. His strength, grace and spirituality are rare and remarkable.

From the vantage point of the flat roof of Nouh's mudbrick home, so reminiscent of the homes of biblical days, we looked across that ancient city, with its aura of history and mystique. We spoke about his work as a pastor, as a shepherd to that tiny flock. "I am here," he said, "to love and to lead this small group of precious people." I asked him whether there were any secret believers among the rest of the population.

"You mean Nicodemuses?" he asked.

"There are many of them. They are secret disciples, who seek after Jesus, yet find it impossible to break with the cultural and social strength of Islam. I am here to care for and to love them as well."

He took us to a few huge 'open' wells on the outskirts of the city. These wells of Timbuktu are not normal wells, small in diameter, from which water is winched to the surface in a bucket or other receptacle. Timbuktu's open wells resemble immense inverted conical pits, many hundreds of feet in diameter at the top, narrowing down to a small central hole in the bottom into which water seeps from an underground source. The pool of water at the bottom was brown and muddy.

Thousands of steps and small areas of garden were cut into the sloping walls of these deep conical pits. The well we visited was a hive of activity. Dozens of men and women, carrying buckets, pots or skin receptacles, were continually running down the steps, collecting the precious water to carry it up to the small terraced gardens for which each of them was responsible. They were tending, with great care, various types of vegetables and edible plants, crucial for survival.

1987 was 'survival time' in Timbuktu! Famine of devastating proportions had ravaged equatorial Africa from west to east. Tens of thousands had died, and millions more were under the threat of death, as seasonal rains yielded to the relentless sun that dried up the land. As in so many other natural disasters like this, the services of MAF were life-saving. We provided transportation of relief supplies and gave mobility to the many people who came to help. It was a special privilege to be at the centre of such an outpouring of compassion.

Our new-found pastor friend wanted Jo and me to visit the cemetery at Timbuktu. Cemeteries are not usually on the 'must do' list for us. But we acceded to his continuing request that we go there. I look back now upon that visit with profound gratitude for what I was about to see and experience.

The cemetery at Timbuktu was unlike any I had ever seen. There were no headstones, no identifying plaques. This was no lawn cemetery. Indeed, there were no real graves. It appeared akin to a place I knew only in the recesses of my imagination – the valley of dry bones – from Ezekiel 37. The scene was macabre. Bones, bleached by the burning sun, littered the entire area. Line after line of bare white skulls, each with a deathly grin, clearly marked the peculiar regimented rows of this strange, ancient graveyard.

The sands of the lower Sahara, like the dunes of a lonely foreshore, are constantly on the move, driven by strong, hot desert winds. Bodies buried beneath the sand soon, sometimes too soon, emerge from below to become skeletons littering the landscape of this burial ground.

Strangely, mixed with the regimented lines of bleached human remains were pieces of pottery. Some, on older graves, were small, crumbly orange-coloured shards worn smooth by the relentless winds. On the newer graves, more gruesome-looking with their blowing remnants of shroud material slowly disintegrating in the scorching sun, the pottery pieces were sharper, newer and larger. I could see they were the remnants of large water pots, like those I'd seen in the houses of Timbuktu.

It was a strange and eerie place. Jo and I were deeply affected by the experience. We were aware at some indefinable level that there was a significant reason for us being there that day. As we walked through the lines of bones, I asked Nouh about the broken pottery pieces. He explained, "It is the custom of the people here, that when a body is buried, a pot is placed on the grave, then ceremonially broken to signify, with deep sadness, that, forever, life has drained away into the sand."

Standing there in a valley of dry bones, surrounded by the stark and chilling evidence of the hopelessness of death without Christ, we became poignantly aware of the presence of God to a degree we have seldom experienced. Passages from Scripture, some of them words of Jesus Himself, came to my mind as if spoken by God Himself.

"I, even I, am the Lord and apart from me there is no saviour."

"I am the way and the truth and the life. No-one comes to the Father except through me."

"He who has the son has life. He who does not have the Son of God does not have life."

It was a memorable experience. There was no 'burning bush'. There was no audible voice. But I felt we stood on holy ground, a place of profound challenge. We were in the company of this superb young man of Mali, a man of God. And God was there. In this remote desert cemetery, we felt Him leading us, beckoning us on, challenging us to respond to this world of need where in so many places 'life is draining away into the sand.'

Later that day we drove out over the dunes of the Sahara to meet a group of people with whom Pastor Nouh was working. These were the legendary Berbers of the desert. Dignified and beautiful people, they carried an unmistakable air of nobility. I had read of their independence and their strength of character. They were cattle people of the desert. Their wealth had been in the herds of cattle and goats they drove from place to place in their nomadic wandering. But no cattle were left. Their goats had also been a traditional source of food and milk, their skins providing covering and protection. But there had been years of terrible drought. No goats were left. They had nothing. Now in the throes of famine, they were hanging on with desperation to the last vestiges of self-sufficiency and pride. They were hurting, disenfranchised and on the brink of extinction. What is more, they seemed totally broken in spirit.

Now forced to abandon a nomadic way of life and settle in one place, they were enduring the ignominy of being 're-acculturated'. They were learning how to garden, to grow food in the ground, and to stay there long enough for it to produce. As a part of the international effort and outpouring of compassion for Mali's suffering, a deep-shaft well had been dug for them from which they were able to draw water for their small, square garden plots in the sand. As they poured this meagre water supply from the goatskin buckets on to the rows of little plants, patting up the sandy sides of each area so the water couldn't escape, they looked more like sad children playing games on a seaside beach than noble cattlemen of the desert.

It was a heart-wrenching sight. Hungry, pitifully thin, they were wrapped in dark desert robes. I could only see black hands, faces and piercing black eyes. Their long-term survival seemed unlikely.

The women and children were sitting in the shade of inadequate shelters, skin-covered frameworks of sticks providing little protection from the blistering rays of the sun. I felt an overwhelming sense of frustration that I, personally, could do so little for them on that day. We gave them the grain we had brought in the truck, but that was barely a short-term solution. What would their tomorrow bring? With a troubled heart I walked alone around those simple huts.

Looking into these eyes filled with overwhelming sadness and hopelessness, I understood why my staff, even the tough ones, in their reports back to my office had spoken so often of their own tears and of the almost unbearable emotional pressure of working among these people.

I found myself humming a little song. My surprise was not that I was humming. I often do that. It was rather the particular song that had subconsciously come to my mind. Just as the bones and the pottery of the morning's visit to the cemetery had been used to speak to me a profound message, so did this little song in the afternoon hours in that heartbreaking environment of thirst and death.

I've got a river of life flowing out of me, makes the lame to walk and the blind to see, opens prison doors, sets the captives free, I've got a river of life flowing out of me.[1]

These people desperately needed the generous help of overseas governments and aid organisations in digging wells and sending other assistance. They needed even their impossible dream of another breed of cattle able to survive the rigours of the Sahara Desert that could return their culture to them. They needed the grain we carried. They needed loving hands to dispense those life-saving things.

"I've got a river of life flowing out of me."

More than anything else they needed that 'stream of living water' that Jesus says flows from the innermost being of those who truly believe in Him.

That 'living water' is ours to give.

Timbuktu. What a name. It is not an imaginary place, a fantasy in a small boy's story book. It is a wonderful, unique, ancient city of rich culture – and the parish of one of the finest young men I have ever met.

Note
1. I've got a River of Life. L Casebolt

24

An Albanian Named Jimmy

So from Jerusalem all the way round to Illyricum, I have
fully proclaimed the gospel of Christ. It has always been
my ambition to preach the gospel where Christ was not
known.

Romans 15:19–20

'Jimmy' was from Albania. To this day, I don't know his real
name. He told me one day, but he laughed as I tried to
pronounce it. "Forget it," he said. "It's an Albanian name.
Anything to do with Albania only brings sadness and pain.
Just call me Jimmy."

So Jimmy he was. And I loved him.

The year was 1977. We met in an orthopaedic ward of a
Melbourne hospital. Both of us were trussed up like chickens
at the time in 'seven-pound traction', a sadistically designed
instrument of torture for the treatment of the spinal disc
problem we each had. Heavy weights attached to our legs
with an apparatus of cords and pulleys were intended to
'stretch' us back into shape! So there we lay, captive audience
to one another. For hours we talked, often through the long
hours of the night, sharing stories.

It was hard to believe the things he told me about Albania.
My knowledge of his strange and secretive homeland was

very scanty. I knew that Russia had been considered too liberal for the Albanian leadership, which then made friends with China. It had been the only nation in the world to declare itself atheistic and was brutal to any of its citizens who broke the laws banning religion.

Jimmy's life in Albania had left scars on his heart. Nevertheless, he had probably been as much a problem to the authorities as they had been to him. He was a 'lovable rascal' with a twinkle in his eye! He wrought havoc among the nurses, indiscreetly taunting and provoking them. They scolded him continuously, often with blushes of embarrassment at his jokes and language, which were colourful to say the least. He had acquired his English in a decidedly rough and uncouth environment. But those nurses loved him as much as I did.

There was no twinkle in his eye, however, when he told me of his last night in Albania. He described how he had gone down to the beach, looked back at the land of his birth, and muttered to himself, "I would rather die than stay here." And taking off his clothes, he had swum out into the ocean in the darkness.

But Jimmy found freedom the next day. Some distance out on the Adriatic and clinging to a length of floating timber, he was rescued by the crew of an Italian fishing boat. He claimed asylum in Italy and, in time, began a new life in Australia as a political refugee.

Jimmy, in the dark of night, sometimes cried.

I longed to introduce him to Jesus. Occasionally, I read to him from the Bible. And sometimes he would shed tears of gratitude when I prayed for him, for his land and his people.

I never led him to Christ. Yielding didn't come easily to him. And eventually I was released from the hospital. When I returned, as soon as I was able to visit him, I found that he too had been discharged – and was gone. I traced his address and went there, hoping to find him. He had disappeared.

I never saw Jimmy again.

Many times since over the years, I have thought about him. I have often found myself driving by the simple rooming house in Melbourne where he had lived. I have prayed, as I do still, that wherever Jimmy is, God would protect my dear friend. And perhaps lead him to that place where there is to be no more tears.

Jimmy left me a legacy of love. A love for him and for his homeland. That strange Balkan nation had somehow become very significant in my heart and thinking, although my faith was too small even to imagine that I would ever visit there. It was a closed and mysterious country.

Eventually, however, things changed. In 1985, Enver Hoxha, Albania's communist dictator, died. Control passed into other hands, equally as hard. They too ruled with iron fists and kept the doors firmly shut to the outside world. But the world, and even Albania, was changing.

Sitting at my desk in Redlands, California, my thoughts often turned to Albania. It remained separated from the rest of the world behind walls of oppression and godlessness. I prayed for the people, as I had done many times, that they someday would have the opportunity in freedom and openness to learn about the God who loved them. I took a file from my drawer. The tab said 'Albania'. I read again the material I had gathered over the years and placed it back in the cabinet under A.

In the early nineties, what had seemed entirely impossible became reality! The dividing wall had come down in Germany. The USSR had begun to crumble. Totalitarian communism was dying. And its demise heralded the threshold to freedom for the people of those ancient lands struggling to loosen their bonds and begin a new way of life.

The domino effect was sweeping and immediate. Freedom was even on the horizon for Albania. And in that ancient land, known in Bible times as Illyricum, the ancient door began to creak open.

Then one day in 1990 as I prayed, with my now fat Albania file open before me on my desk, the phone rang.

It was a man totally unknown to me. But he was calling to ask whether I would consider being a part of a small delegation. A delegation to enter Albania! Of all places.

Because of other commitments, and much to my disappointment, I had to send someone else. Yet as a result of that visit, MAF USA became a leading player, from the outset, in the establishment of the new evangelistic thrust in that Balkan nation.

And when finally, in 1991, I descended the steps of a Swiss-Air DC-9 and stepped on to Albanian soil, it was a moment of profound joy and poignant memory. Jimmy's homeland.

"Anything to declare?" This familiar question came not from a sophisticated customs officer but from a rather diminutive middle-aged lady dressed in an oversized khaki-coloured army greatcoat buttoned up to the neck. The red star on her cap needed a polish.

"No," I said as I walked by her. I had nothing to declare.

My first impression of Albania was of the tangible fear under which its people lived. Thousands of dome-shaped concrete bunkers, gun emplacements, were randomly positioned along the roadside, like giant mushrooms in the fields. They were even between houses. Now empty, they had once been occupied by conscripted militiamen who had lived an abiding but deliberately perpetrated fear that 'the Americans were coming to destroy them!'

As I stood on the roof of the Tirana hotel at 6:00am the following morning, I looked down upon the city square.

Thousands of people made their way to work. All I could hear was the slapping sound of shoes against the pavement, but no other noise. There were no vehicles. Not even the sound of soft human voices drifting up to me from below. Just the sound of people walking.

Albanians didn't talk to strangers. People were not to be trusted.

In the depth of the soul of this people was a vast, deep void. And it was strangely familiar. Something was missing. I had seen it before . . . all those years ago, in a Melbourne hospital room.

But fear was in retreat in Albania. The sense of anticipation and hope was unmistakable. A new wind was blowing. A new light was dawning upon the nation's darkened soul. On the day before my arrival in Tirana, thousands of angry but triumphant students had toppled the statue of Enver Hoxha that had stood for generations in the city square.

The air of triumph was most manifest at the 'Freedom Concert' I attended in Tirana's city hall. The roar of applause from the mainly student audience was electrifying as they yelled their appreciation and expressed their national pride as they listened to the old Albanian folk songs and watched the dances. There were many tears of joy in that place that night. Sitting through that superb concert, I felt almost like an intruder. The night belonged to Albania, to Albanians, not to casual visitors from the West to enjoy. The night belonged to Jimmy. I wished he had been there with me.

On a visit to Skodra, Albania's northernmost city, I met a man who was exactly my age. We had been born within a few days of each other in 1935. Our lives, however, had been lived in vastly different ways. I thought about my life of freedom, of ease and comfort, of travel and excitement as he told me about his. He had been put into prison with his entire aristocratic family when he was nine years old! Nine years old! For almost forty-seven years he had been deprived of basic personal freedom. Upon his release, just a short time before our arrival, what remained of his old family estate had been returned to him.

So I visited this man in his once-magnificent mansion. It was now almost lost in the mass of crudely constructed high-density housing pressing right up against its walls. A beautiful mosaic sidewalk created by a master craftsman more than a century ago and which had formally meandered through the expansive grounds and gardens, was barely discernable in a few places between the masses of rundown dwellings. As this man, the grandson of a former prince of the Balkans, sat in one of the only two habitable rooms of that grand old home, he said, with no sign of emotion whatsoever, "And now I am free."

It seemed as if the ability to understand or express the concept of freedom had been lost behind all the razor wire of forty-seven years.

Jimmy had achieved freedom by placing his life at risk. This man had been finally granted his freedom. But for both Jimmy and this aristocratic man of Skodra, there was another kind of freedom. It was a freedom about which neither of them knew anything at all.

And as I had told Jimmy in that hospital bed so many years before, I again struggled to tell this man in Skodra about that other freedom available to him, the freedom of the soul. Spiritual freedom. That spiritual freedom is not achieved by risking one's life, or by swimming into the darkness, or even by the opening of prison gates. This freedom is lasting and indestructible. And it is available to all who will accept it, through the One who gently and lovingly says, "If the Son sets you free, you will be free indeed."

In 1990, we knew of only about thirty Christians in Albania. But the beginnings of spiritual freedom were evident nonetheless. Deeply dedicated people were coming from all points of the globe to share God's love. I went to church in the sitting room of an old stone house not far from the centre of Tirana.

There was no noticeboard, no stained glass, very little furniture, no pulpit. There were no well-dressed people there. There was no church bulletin and no ordained preacher. A young, Italian-speaking man from Switzerland in his early twenties was their pastor.

These Albanian Christ-followers didn't know how to 'do church'! These were people who were just passionately in love with Jesus! And there, I saw 'joy unspeakable'. This joy lit up the faces of the few Albanians who were there in a way I had never seen. As they worshipped, I was brought to tears.

God had not abandoned these people. No godless dictator and his evil regime had eradicated God from this nation. Perhaps one might say Hoxha was almost successful. Yes, there was little understanding of God's love in Albania in those early nineties. Only the old could remember. Anyone younger than forty-seven years would only have been told of God in absolute secrecy. It seemed as if the very soul of the nation had been taken almost to the brink of destruction.

But only to the brink!

A couple of times I sat in the lobby of the Hotel Tirana and made sure there was an empty chair by my side. Within minutes, someone would come and ask, with typical Albanian courtesy, "May I sit by you?" Then, every time, the same questions would come. Phrased differently? Perhaps. But the same. A longing of soul.

"Are you from the West?"

"May I speak with you about life outside Albania?"

"Who is God? Is He real? Does He really care about us? Is there any hope? What is the Church? Can it help us find a new dignity?"

As I was driven to Tirana's international airport some days later, I remembered the khaki-coated lady who had greeted me upon arrival. I could still hear her question, "Anything to declare?"

I looked for her but couldn't find her. I wanted to tell her, "Yes! Yes! I do have something to declare!" This was no trite item that would attract duty! This was without price but beyond value. And I longed to tell her.

The Psalmist tells us, "Declare his glory among the nations, his marvellous deeds among all peoples." That is the declaration we make to the nation of Albania.

Since those early days, the people of God from the free world have with great clarity and effectiveness made that declaration in Albania.

Today, there are not so many foreigners in Albania. It's a good thing. The new Albanian church that came to birth in the agony of a disenfranchised and oppressed people is strong. It is withstanding the predictable pressure of entry into the world of capitalism. It doesn't need so many outsiders now. Predictably, some new believers have drifted away, but there are thousands who remain firm in their new-found faith.

I visited Albania again in June 1999, this time at the invitation of the association of evangelical churches. In 1990 there were less than fifty believers there. Nine years later I spoke to pastors and leaders representing more than one hundred and sixty churches.

The touch of God has been upon that land in the decade of the nineties. Miracles have happened. Lives have been transformed. People have been empowered as a church has been born. It is a church that, though young in experience and in years, is vitally alive and gloriously enthusiastic. The experience of hearing them sing, of sensing their joy, and feeling their irrepressible spirit will remain one of the highlights of my life.

At the time of my visit in 1999, Albania was caught in the midst of the terrible ethnic and cultural crisis between the Serbs of Yugoslavia and the ethnic Albanians of Kosovo. More than four hundred thousand ethnic Albanians had fled south from Kosovo to Albania, seeking safety. Refugee camps were established all over the country, some as 'tent cities' in the countryside, some occupying long-derelict buildings in Albanian towns and cities. Kosovar lives had been shattered as the Yugoslavian military seemed to have been given the freedom to do their worst among them. Stories of ethnic cleansing, of rape, pillage and murder were rife among these refugee people.

International relief agencies flooded into Albania. The international airport looked like a war zone with aircraft of all shapes and sizes crowding its tarmac and aprons. Military forces from major European nations and the USA built their own tent cities in the area. Large transport aircraft brought food and other material aid to these deprived and disenfranchised refugees. At night the noise of high-flying NATO fighter planes and bombers was a constant drone as they flew across Albania to drop their destructive payloads on Yugoslavian targets.

And where was this young, enthusiastic Albanian church at this time of pressure and tension?

The church was in the refugee camps, ministering to the grieving, to the lost, to the hurting ethnic Albanians of Kosovo who had come seeking refuge. Along with food, clothing and encouragement, these refugees from the north who were mainly Muslim in faith received the Good News of Jesus Christ! Muslim refugees, astounded at the love shown by their Albanian Christian brothers and sisters, flocked into the churches of Albania. They could not believe that people could be so loving, so caring.

Church leaders were making plans, deciding which of their

people would go with the refugees back to Kosovo when they were able to return home. These new relationships were seen as a God-given challenge to continue to share their faith with the Kosavars – in Kosovo. This was to be their first missionary endeavour – and they were not going to miss the opportunity. God's opportunity.

The nurses in Mitcham Private Hospital in Melbourne would never agree, but I think, in a way, Jimmy was a kind of angel! He came into my life just for three short weeks. But he was used of God to open my mind and prepare me for an appointment some fourteen years later. Through a trussed-up friend, carrying a heart full of pain, God planted a seed that would spring to life and bear much fruit.

Makes you think about 'casual' acquaintances, doesn't it?

I wish I knew where Jimmy was today.

25

War

He makes wars cease to the ends of the earth; he breaks the bow and shatters the spear, he burns the shields with fire. "Be still, and know that I am God; I will be exalted among the nations, I will be exalted in the earth."

Psalm 46:9–10

In the early sixties, Jo and I, with our two small boys, lived in a very small aluminium house right on the edge of the beach at Wewak, Papua New Guinea. We would walk along the sand. And often, after a storm, we'd see them. Rolling around in the surf, or left at the high-tide mark. Human bones. Perhaps a femur, or a tibia, a scapula, or a curved bone of the rib cage. The fury of a tropical storm would wrest them out of their secret watery graves and deposit them on the sands of Wewak's beaches.

There, above the tideline, we would dig a hole and bury them.

Whose bones were they?

Did they belong to someone we knew?

The father, perhaps, of a childhood friend?

American? Australian? Perhaps Japanese? We couldn't tell. But this we did know. Some young man, long ago, had set out from a distant home to fight for a cause – and never returned.

A relative of Jo's had been shot down over the sea there in Wewak, towards the last days of the war. His commanding officer had written to the family, describing his bravery as a fighter pilot. "I saw his plane take a hit over Wewak, and I watched it crash into the bay," he wrote. He had been twenty-one years old. Perhaps we had buried one of his bones.

On Saturday afternoons, we would take the kids to a beach called Moem, a few miles to the east. With face mask and snorkel, we would swim for hours in the warm waters of our own tropical aquarium, just a few feet from the shore. The vivid colours of the schools of fish enhanced the spectacular beauty of the coral reefs that paralleled the beach. It was an exotic place, peaceful and secluded.

One particular Saturday, in the late sixties, as we were relaxing there, Michael, Timothy, Jonathon and Robin hassled us to allow them to go and 'explore'. The jungle nearby was thick, almost impenetrable, and grew to the water's edge.

Our children were very much at home in the jungle, so we agreed, but with the strong proviso that they go no further than shouting distance. But within a few minutes they bounded out of the bush, wildly excited.

To our amazement and horror, they were carrying belts of still-live World War II ammunition. They also had a number of personal identification 'dog tags'.

"The bullets and these things were all mixed up with the bones," said Michael, our oldest, panting. They led me impatiently to the site of the find.

There, just yards from our picnic site, was the wreckage of what had been a B-24 Liberator bomber. It had lain where it had crashed, hidden for a quarter of a century in the ever-enveloping jungle undergrowth.

With the kids, I sifted through the pieces. Among the broken metal and shards of sun-baked perspex, lay the scattered, whitened bones of the crew.

Who were these men? We talked together about them.

They were men who had loved and had been loved. They were MIAs – missing in action – their loss made all the more poignant because their bodies had never been found. Somebody's sons. Somebody's husbands. Somebody's brothers. Their families had never known how they died or where. Maybe their children still lived in the United States but had no memory of their fathers. Just stories.

When the ID tags and remains were eventually returned to their homeland, undoubtedly, to some degree for the families of the men, there was closure. Perhaps there were official burials in veterans' cemeteries in the United States. Healing tears were shed, I'm sure, as honour was given to those men, lost for so many years.

It was simply a routine operation. To dig a ditch.

But once again, they were there. In the ditch. The national workers found them. Human bones. This time, though, in a line of unmarked graves. It was immediately apparent that these bodies had been haphazardly, even violently, thrown into the ground. There was no dignity. They were not lying in any orderly, respectful way. Each rough grave contained just a mixed-up mess of bones, piled on top of one another. But no skulls. Not one. Each skeleton was without a head. And so they remained, totally unidentifiable, lost victims of a gruesome wartime execution!

Our family was living in Wewak in 1970 when the celebration of the twenty-fifth anniversary of the Japanese surrender to the Allied forces took place. A few miles away, Wom Point had been one of the sites where formal signings of surrender took place. There, at Wom, a white obelisk marked the place where the commanding general of the Japanese forces of the region handed over his sword to the Allied commander.

Hundreds of veterans came from all over the world to commemorate the anniversary. Americans, Australians and Japanese. And one single man from India. He was the sole survivor of an entire Indian battalion that had been captured on the Malay Peninsula and brought by the Japanese all the way to Papua New Guinea to serve them. At liberation, there were eighteen Indian soldiers left. All of them, save this one man, who was ill at the time, were being transported by air to Rabaul to join a ship back to India when their plane crashed. All were killed.

And so, here, twenty-five years later, former enemies reminisced quietly together. And reconciled. Twenty-five years had brought a lot of healing.

I talked to one middle-aged Japanese lady standing at the periphery of the crowd. She pointed to an area of heaped, crushed coral. "My husband . . . buried here . . . ," she said in her broken English. Then she looked up and, pointing to fourteen-month-old Chris, sitting on my shoulders, she said, "My son . . . little . . . like him . . . when daddy go away. He not remember." But she remembered.

The rivers of Gaudalcanal 'ran red with blood' in World War II. I have waded through those rivers and flown over them many times. The Solomon Island people living there had no war of their own. It was a war between other nations, but fought on their land. Their country and villages were devastated. Thousands were killed, and their peaceful way of life was forever changed.

At another place and time of remembrance I visited Gettysburg. Walking in the stillness and silence along the lines of canon that remain in the fields there, I read the plaques. Each one outlined the history of a battle. I felt an almost overwhelming sense of sadness at the thought of the hundreds of thousands of men and women who died in those dark and dreadful days of civil war – all of them Americans.

It seemed that I could almost hear the stirring words of Abraham Lincoln:

> Fourscore and seven years ago our fathers brought forth on this continent, a new nation, conceived in Liberty, and dedicated to the proposition that all men are created equal. Now we are engaged in a great civil war, testing whether that nation, or any nation so conceived and so dedicated, can long endure . . . But in a larger sense, we cannot dedicate – we cannot consecrate – we cannot hallow – this ground. The brave men, living and dead, who struggled here, have consecrated it, far above our poor power to add or detract . . .

Gettysburg, today, is not only a moving and sensitively presented national cemetery; it is a constant reminder to the American people that civil war must never be allowed to happen again. Never!

It was January 1995. We were driven up the steep, rocky road from Peshawar, Pakistan, through the Khyber Pass into Afghanistan. Rudyard Kipling seemed to speak from every rock, every hill. From a cramped position in an overcrowded minibus there was a panorama across the brown, dry mountains to the faraway peaks of the famed Hindu Kush. But as I looked down into the ravines and canyons, I saw the rusted remains of hundreds of trucks, tanks and other pieces of military equipment. Afghanistan had been a war zone for generations.

In the streets of Kabul, rows of deserted, ruined buildings bore their own terrible scars of war – holes blasted in thick reinforced concrete, twisted steel girders, empty window frames. I met and shared food with wonderful Afghani people. The children and most of the adults have only known a life of conflict, danger and pain. The very fabric of the life of Afghanistan is permeated with effects of war. So many have been 'child soldiers'.

Far too many children today bear arms instead of toys. One, just one, is too many. It must be one of the greatest human rights offences of modern times. I have seen children, barely in their teens, being driven along dusty roads, uniformed soldiers, with oversized metal helmets too heavy to bear, pressed into active service, desperately trying to look older than their years. They are trained to kill and destroy. They know how to use the sophisticated weaponry they carry. Their childhood has been stolen from them, never to be returned. Years, which should contain fun, learning and joy, have been taken away. What a perversion of the carefree innocence of all that God meant childhood to be.

Scripture, too, talks of war. Another kind of warfare.

And the people of God today, as they have been throughout time, are involved in this warfare. It is not warfare of nation against nation, of guns and missiles and bombs. It is not fought in the physical realm. But it is warfare, nonetheless. It is spiritual warfare, where the powers of God are arrayed against the powers of evil. Where hope is arrayed against despair.

Looking back on the seasons of my life, I see interesting contrasts and comparisons. My Air Force logbook records three thousand flights. My MAF logbook records more than thirty thousand. In my days of military aviation I helped refine the tools of war, working with the brightest of human minds involved in weapons research. In my days of mission aviation I became involved in that other kind of warfare, the battle for the souls of men.

MAF pilots don't fire guns or rockets. They don't drop bombs. They don't wreak havoc and devastation. But there is a cost. And sometimes the cost is life itself.

There is one remarkable difference.

This war is not just winnable. Its victory is absolute and certain.

> *But thanks be to God! He gives us the victory through our Lord Jesus Christ.*
>
> 1 Corinthians 15:57

26

Foundations

*For no-one can lay any foundation other than the one
already laid, which is Jesus Christ.*

1 Corinthians 3:11

"I don't know where it is, Michael, but it must be somewhere
near here."

We were forcing our way through tropical growth between
the road from the beach, about thirty yards away. It grabbed
at our sweaty skin and our clothes. The ground underfoot was wet and soft. Vines, creepers and succulent plants
surrounded us, up to six or seven feet high. The brilliant
sapphire-coloured sea, just beyond the low sandy dunes, was
mirror-like, visible through the undergrowth and tall coconut
palms. Although the sea was calm, like shiny, rich blue glass,
tiny waves made soft swishing sounds as they broke lazily
upon the grey sand.

It was so hot. So humid. So very – Wewak.

At that latitude, almost on the equator, the sun shines
fiercely from directly overhead. Nothing alleviated the heavy
pall of tropical heat and humidity that dragged the sweat
out of our bodies in balls upon our foreheads and in rivulets
down our backs.

This was August 2000, and my eldest son, Michael, and I

were trying to find the place where our house had stood when we first came to Papua New Guinea in 1961. We had just flown in from Mount Hagen and decided to look for our old home before we did anything else. We crossed the road between the airstrip and the small settlement of national houses scattered around the area where our house had been.

"Everything looks so small after thirty years, Dad," Michael remarked in a surprised voice. "I guess I was just a little kid then."

The house was no longer standing. We hadn't expected to find it, anyway. But the foundation, a two-foot-thick cement slab, should surely be there, somewhere.

Two or three men and a woman stood watching us. Obviously they wondered what on earth two white strangers were doing poking around their village and trying to force a way into the heavy bushes nearby.

We used the old airfield hangar as a reference point, but uncurbed tropical growth had totally changed the landscape. Nothing was recognisable. Eventually, behind a yellow-painted wooden trade store building, we found a single old cement slab. At one time it had obviously been the foundation of something. *"Mi harim tok, bipo dispela em i haus bilong ol contrak,"* one of the men said. ("I've heard that long ago this was a house for plantation contract workers.")

In 1961 there had been an ex-World War II Quonset hut where primitive bushmen from distant areas were accommodated. They had been recruited to work in the copra plantations on the outer islands of Papua New Guinea. Sometimes they stayed for weeks in Wewak, waiting for a chartered DC-3 to take them to their destinations. Most of them had never seen a car, a road, the sea – and certainly not a white woman.

This was our answer. It was the clue we needed.

This dome-shaped corrugated metal hut had been barely fifty feet from our house.

"That means that the foundation of our place must be in the middle of that heavy stuff over there," we said to each other as we launched off into the even thicker undergrowth.

And there it was!

Hidden inside a dense mass of bushes, creepers and vines was the clear outline of a building. It was obviously the old cement slab. But now it was a dense mass, about twelve inches deep, of succulent leaves. Creepers and vines of all sorts completely covered it. They had gradually enveloped it as the years had passed. All signs of the structure had long since gone. But not the foundation!

It was the floor plan of our house, without a doubt. In rich, verdant green.

I scrambled up on to the slab and stood there remembering.

Thirty-nine years, almost to the day, slipped away. I was walking into the house for the first time, with Jo and seventeen-month-old Michael. We had been driven a number of miles out of the small town of Wewak along a dusty road in MAF's World War II jeep. "No other white people live out here," we were told. I had tried not to show my shock and horror when I saw where we would be living. Little more than a shed, unlined and constructed of thin, heat-attracting silver aluminium. Partitions of the same material formed a main bedroom barely large enough for the double bed. There were two even smaller bedrooms, one containing a single bed and the other, a 'meat-safe' cot.

The house had no regular windows. Each room had one four-foot length of the exterior cladding, hinged at the top, that could be propped open with a stick. But no fly wire to stop the invading hordes of anopheles mosquitoes, all ready and waiting to share the malaria they carried. The roof was formed of sheets of this Kingstrand aluminium. These were held together with rows of small bolts and nuts that in the extreme heat of midday would 'pop' right out. When the first inevitable rainstorms came later that night, we realised that we were living in something resembling a giant, upturned colander.

Wall-to-wall carpet was very fashionable in those days. We had wall-to-wall malthoid, a building material composed of pitch-impregnated paper. Someone had thoughtfully laid it over the rough cement to which it had firmly attached itself. Within a few moments of our arrival that first day, our white-skinned Michael in his white, cloth nappies, resembled a Dalmatian. We found to our dismay that the tar melted in the heat and adhered permanently to feet, shoes, clothes and anything else that came into contact with it. We tried many times to remove that charming black wall-to-wall floor covering. Unsuccessfully. It's probably still there, under the updated carpet of green leaves.

The side entrance to the house was via an upturned wooden crate. There was no electricity. It was miles from town. No other white people lived so far out.

What a dwelling place! Why, then, were Michael and I so anxious to find where it had been? Why? Because the fifteen months we'd spent there had indelibly printed upon our minds the most amazing and unique memories. Humorous and hilarious, horrible and hard, hazardous and humiliating – but above all, happy, happy memories.

I stepped on to what had been the floor of our tiny kitchen. I pictured my beautiful, young, six-months-pregnant wife, fresh from her comfortable, upper-class home in Adelaide as she struggled to cook on a two-burner, kerosene 'wick' stove. Often it refused to light. Mostly it went out almost immediately, anyway. There was no oven. We didn't need one. The whole house was a giant oven!

I walked over to where the living area had been. It doubled as a dining room, barely large enough for the long table with a bench down each side. I remembered the meals we ate there in the light of our one pressure lamp, and vividly recalled the intense pain of the third-degree burns I received to my arm when the lamp exploded as I was lighting it three days after our arrival. I had to hitch a ride to the Wewak hospital in the town's one and only taxi that, miraculously, was passing by right at that time. We didn't even know the town had a taxi! Jo and Michael were left alone in pitch darkness.

Moving a few feet, I stood where our double bed had been. Memories came tumbling into my mind.

– The six-foot-long snake we discovered in the beam of our flashlight that first night. It had taken up residence on top of the aluminium wall above the bed.

– Jo opting to walk along the dark road to a distant house for help while I babysat the reptile. We had absolutely no idea what to do. Many were the subsequent stories about the new MAF pilot who couldn't even kill a snake.

– Sitting on the bed with guests, crammed together under the enormous superfine mosquito net, eating dinner, playing cards, laughing uproariously, and drawing straws to see who would brave the sandfly and mosquito hordes to go and make a cup of tea! After dusk, inside the net on the double bed was the only bug-free haven we had.

– Lying in bed listening to the roaring of the surf crashing on the beach a few yards away, and hearing the reverberations as violent tropical thunderstorms rattled the entire house and lightning illuminated the silver walls.

– Trying to decide whether to close the shutters against the driving rain and stifle, or open them and get wet.

– Tending to Tim, our tiny, sickly baby born in January 1962, whose little crib stood in the makeshift wardrobe in the corner of the room. Wardrobe? It was merely a piece of three-by-three plywood suspended from the ceiling. There was a broom handle from one corner to the other where we normally hung our clothes. That is, when Tim wasn't using it as his personal shelter! It effectively kept the drips off him whenever it rained.

I took a few more paces to where Michael's small bedroom had been and remembered the horror we felt on the morning we discovered that during the night rats had gnawed every casein button off his pyjama top. There was disgust mixed with amusement on another morning when we found him pushing his little toy boat around the bedroom in three inches of water. He had loaded it with 'cargo', he told us. The long brown object in it had floated in with the king tide during the night. The transit contract workers who lived in the Quonset hut next door had no toilet facilities except the bushes. Anything deposited there was flushed out in the gently swirling waters and frequently floated into our house through the spaces under the doors and walls. Our slab, of course, was at ground level. On an exceptionally high tide or in a big storm, there was no escaping the water that flowed over the sand hill and into our small depression. Sometimes it was two feet deep in the yard . . . and six inches deep throughout the house.

Nearby national houses were built on stilts, their floors well above water level. This also made them much more comfortable. They caught even the slightest breeze from the ocean. We, on the other hand, were denied this luxury in our hot little hollow.

Michael and I stepped across to stand on the shape of the old front porch. The slab is lower there, where the ground slopes upwards a few feet to the road. We saw an enormous frangipani tree just to the right. It overhangs the road and is covered with fragrant pink and white blossoms. "We planted that," I exclaimed to Michael with surprise and delight. "It was just a scraggy, two-foot-long shoot when we stuck it in the ground." I wondered whether Jo's red salvia plants were still growing. She had planted them outside the front door. They were brilliantly colourful after a good rain. The rest of the time they were grey-green, as was everything else in the vicinity, including the contents of the house. Clouds of pervasive white crushed coral dust from the road a few feet away filled the air with each passing vehicle. But I saw no red salvia in the dense bush.

A power pole still stood there. I wondered if it was the same one that had been erected all those years ago. I relived the excitement of that memorable day. We had been without electricity for more than six months, but finally the power was on! A heavy black cable, like a huge umbilical cord, was fed through the gap between the wall and the roof. It was suspended across the middle of the 'living' room and anchored on the far wall. We attached to it a proliferation of double adapters, one upon the other upon the other, like some grotesque tree! Extension cords snaked all over the house. We had light. We had power for a frying pan. We had fans! Luxury living – provided there was no power failure.

But there is a downside to everything. The prolific, large grey rats in the area, who insisted on sharing our house, found the long, hanging wire a marvellous place to perform their tightrope walking skills, especially after dark. I can still hear the terrified shriek of an overnight guest whom we had neglected to inform about our furry friends. "Yikes!" she screamed at about 1:00am when she encountered a troupe of them practising their balancing act on the high wire. In the light of her flashlight, their glaring beady eyes seemed to say, "How dare you invade our domain?" And all she had wanted was a drink of water.

Finally I turned and trod my way over the carpet of thick

vines to the back of the foundation and stood on the very edge. I looked out across the Bismark Sea.

I saw myself a young man again, eagerly kissing my small family goodbye and excitedly leaving to go and fly. To live my dreams. To do what I had known since I was a teenager God had called me to do with my life. For a few moments I stood there quietly.

And then, in my imagination, I see her. Clearly. Now on her own for the day. A slim, tanned young mother, still with her mop of curly blonde hair. She hauls the heavy baby carriage across the creeper-covered dune and drags it through the already hot, soft sand of the beach. A little boy races ahead. His sturdy brown legs are covered with scars and infected sores from multiple mosquito and sandfly bites. They reach the water's edge.

And there she sits, hour after hour, day after endless day, in the shallow, tepid water. Even the continual irritation of sand midges is preferable to the intolerable heat of the metal house in the hollow behind her.

From time to time she takes her frail, fretful baby from his net-enshrouded carriage and nurses him. She has made a simple shelter from the sun for him, using long sticks and a large beach towel. The toddler splashes and plays in the water. *Perhaps he'll be happy for awhile,* she thinks hopefully.

Some distance away a group of brown-skinned children are swimming. Their faint chatter and laughter drift back to her over the long stretch of grey-white sand. A solitary man fishes nearby with a long pole fashioned from the centre rib of a sago palm frond. The shore is littered with flotsam and jetsam. Driftwood. Washed in on the last tide. She sees the branch of a small tree. *I wonder how far that has come,* she thinks. *I wonder what sort of tree it once was.*

The branch has been bleached by the sun, scoured by the sand, washed and scrubbed clean by the tumbling, salty waves. It has no bark, no leaves, no buds, no flowers. It is the bare white skeleton of what was once part of a beautiful tree.

That's just how I feel, she thinks, as she looks at the stark, bare, white branches. *Abandoned, lonely, useless, washed up on an isolated beach. The things that were so precious to me are mostly gone. My friends and family. My career. My music. The comforts of my home. Even my own personal ministry.*

Silent tears roll down her cheeks.

"God," she cries out in her heart. "Where are You? Is this all my missionary service is going to be? Is this why You brought me to this land so far from home?"

And she weeps and weeps.

No one sees. No one knows.

Except God. And He puts His loving arms around her and comforts her.

Jo never let me see the tears she shed there on that lonely beach or in that stifling hot aluminium house. Many years went by before I even heard this story. She was sharing it then with some MAF women.

I write this as a tribute to her courage.

And to the courage of all those other women, her much-loved friends, the wives of my colleagues in MAF.

The old house is gone. But the foundations remain. The memories too. They will never be taken away.

I'm reminded of another foundation.

For years we worked there in that Sepik district of Papua New Guinea. Every morning the quietness and tranquillity of that scene would be shattered by the howling of Cessna engines as we took off to fly out across the mountains.

It was truly a missionary endeavour. People brought a multiplicity of skills and gifts to be used in a joint strategy of evangelism, church planting and holistic development.

Those we served were not exclusively evangelists and preachers by a long shot. Medical doctors, nurses, teachers, agriculturalists, builders, linguists, anthropologists – all were included.

But there was a preponderance of white in that brown country.

More than thirty years later I revisited one of the former major areas of mission activity. In the earlier years, perhaps twenty-five white-skinned men and women would have joyfully welcomed the plane's arrival. But this time, as we landed, there was not a white face to be seen. Everything looked the same. The familiar buildings were still there. I remembered carrying in most of that roofing metal myself in my Cessna 180.

But now it was all brown. There were hundreds of happily smiling national people, eager to shake my hand and greet me on that day.

I had a marvellous conversation with the leader of the church, a man whom I had first met when he was a young Bible college student. I had expected to find that, with the departure of all the missionaries, church numbers would have dwindled. But I was thrilled as he told me a far different story. "There are eighty-five thousand believers in this area," he said, beaming at me. "There is great enthusiasm and life in the church."

"Well, then, how do you now look back on the days when there were so many white missionaries here?" I asked him. His answer thrilled me even more. It affirmed again to me how abundantly worthwhile had been my thirty-seven years in MAF.

"How do I view those days?" He paused a moment. "Let me say just two things," he continued, in his very adequate English. "Firstly, we wouldn't be here as a church if you had not come. Nor would we have been so strong as a people.

Yes, as you say, there were a lot of white skins in those days. We did feel put upon sometimes. We had difficulties dealing with the emergence into the twentieth century. But we thank God for you all, for your coming.

"Secondly," he said, "looking back at the situation as it was then and comparing it to what it is today, I would say this – God used you and our other mission friends to lay a foundation that was to be the basis for His future work. It was on the foundation you laid that God later built the church we have here today!"

Foundations!

I flew away that day with a renewed understanding of the purpose of so much of our service. And a deep thankfulness as I realised in a fresh way the inestimable privilege of being a 'foundation builder'.

That old cement foundation Michael and I so recently walked upon eloquently retold and vividly brought to mind precious personal memories. Yes, the house is gone. But the foundation is standing the test of time. Perhaps someone, some day, will bulldoze it away. It probably won't last forever.

But our memories, and the things we learned in the months we lived there, will last for all time. And that, we now see, was God's divine purpose for our lives.

We learnt about courage, tenacity and commitment. We learnt as well the need for humour and joy. We learnt much about the importance of supportive friends and family, about faith, about caring for and loving one another in a new way. And, oh, how much we learnt about prayer! But mostly we learnt about God and His faithfulness. "I will never leave you or forsake you," He said to us over and over again.

This was the foundation He built *into us* during that time, the qualities and strengths He knew we needed for the years ahead.

Yes, this personal foundation has been buffeted by huge storms. Sometimes it has been submerged by 'king tides'. Its very base has even been threatened with destruction. But it has withstood the test of time. And it still stands today.

And what of that other foundation? The kingdom foundation we were privileged to build? That, especially, will never pass away. Never! No bulldozer can remove it. No one will ever have to force his way through thick jungle to find it. For that foundation, and the house built upon it – the Church – will always stand.

Not even the gates of hell shall prevail against it.

The Builder promised that!

APPENDICES

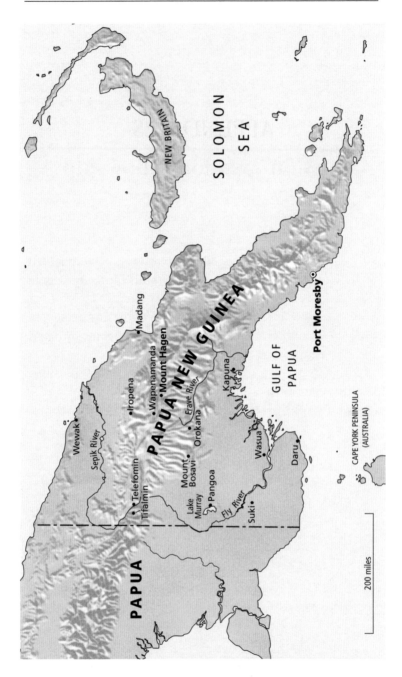

Mission Aviation Fellowship

For over sixty years, pilots like Max Meyers have enabled MAF's ministry to reach out to thousands of needy people across the developing world.

But it takes a team of people to keep pilots and planes in the air, overcoming barriers to bring the Gospel in word and action to people who need it so desperately.

Without supporters like you, none of this would be possible. We want you on our team too.

If you would like to know more, please get in touch with us.

Supporter Relations
Mission Aviation Fellowship UK
Castle Hill Avenue
Folkestone
CT20 2TN

Tel: 0845 850 9505
Email: supporter.relations@maf-uk.org
Website: www.maf-uk.org

Registered charity in England and Wales (1064598) and in Scotland (SC039107)

More stories of adventure and hope . . .

Hope Has Wings is the gripping tale of MAF from 1945 right up to today. Author Stuart King has experienced it all from co-founding MAF in post-war London to the first MAF flight into uncharted Africa. This book will continue to inspire and encourage you long after you've put it down.

Roger Young brings you straight into the joys, trials, horror and humour of being a missionary pilot in *Many Adventures Followed*. He vividly portrays what it was really like in the early years of MAF's service in Papua New Guinea. This is a true story of overcoming adversity and answered prayer.

Jungle Pilot is the story of Nate Saint, a young MAF pilot who was killed along with four other missionaries by the Auca Indians they had gone to serve. As Ted Engstrom of World Vision said, "More than a book about a man and a plane, this is a well-balanced diet of humour, challenge, danger, spiritual power and tragedy turned to triumph."